Sugarbakers' Cookie Cutter
COOKBOOK

Baking and Decorating *Beautiful Cookies* for Every Holiday and Every Season

DIANA COLLINGWOOD BUTTS
AND CAROL V. WRIGHT

Simon & Schuster

SIMON & SCHUSTER
Rockefeller Center
1230 Avenue of the Americas
New York, NY 10020

SIMON & SCHUSTER and colophon are registered trademarks
of Simon & Schuster Inc.

Designed by Deborah Kerner

Manufactured in the United States of America
10   9   8   7   6   5   4   3   2   1

Library of Congress Cataloging-in-Publication Data
Butts, Diana Collingwood.
   Sugarbakers' cookie cutter cookbook : baking and decorating beau-
tiful cookies for every holiday and every season / Diana Collingwood
Butts and Carol V. Wright.
       p.   cm.
   Includes index.
   1. Cookies.   I. Wright, Carol V.   II. Title.
TX772.B88   1997
641.8'654—dc21   97-30673
                                                    CIP

ISBN 0-684-83318-2

FOR JOY DENISON

The only woman I know who loves decorated
cookies as much as I do.
Without your love for and dedication to this
craft, there would be no Sugarbakers'.
You truly are the "Joy" of Cookies.

DIANA

FOR ALICE VON PRESSENTIN COLIN

My mother,
who got me started in the kitchen
and everywhere else.

CAROL

Acknowledgments

First and foremost, our thanks must go to our editor, Sydny Weinberg Miner. Her love for this book was evident from the beginning, and her guiding hand has kept us on course. Thanks also to Monica Gomez for her many hours of work on the project, especially her efforts in unpacking and repacking more than fifty pounds of cookies!

To our agent, Mildred Marmur, and her associate, Jane Lebowitz, for their dedication in finding this book the perfect home.

To our illustrator, Dolores Santoliquido, for making things clear and precise with the stroke of a pen.

To our book designer, Deborah Kerner, and photographer, Ilisa Katz, for capturing the soul of

Sugarbakers' Cookie Cutter Cookbook and getting it down on paper.

To the many hands and minds in the kitchen who worked on the designs and decorated the cookies: Joy Denison of The Joy of Cookies, Kazuko Young, Jody Wagner, Jody Simonson, Kathie Rulon of Sweet Dreams, and Cindy Ousterhout of "O My Goodness!"

To the gifted workers at the tool bench, who perfected and produced beautiful cookie cutters: Dave Denison, Gene Valasek, Rob Wagner, and Patty Bradley of Bark and Bradley.

To our friends in the food industry, without whose help, support, and encouragement this book would not have been possible: the fine people at Wilton Enterprises, Reynolds Aluminum, General

Foods, C & H Sugar, and KitchenAid. Their modern-day equipment makes it possible to turn out sublime cookies.

Last but not least, we wish to thank our families for being involved in the testing, tasting, baking, shopping, and cleaning. To Larry, Lauren, and Keith, who were patient when the only thing to eat in Diana's house was four different kinds of cookies. To Fred and Catherine, who have put on pounds, while Carol proved that by following the directions in this book a writer with intermediate baking skills can turn out delightful, delicious (and delovely) cookies. To neighbors and friends who eagerly critiqued and rated recipes: Round two from Sugarbakers' kitchens will be gooey desserts containing your favorite candy bars. Wanna taste? Come on over!

—DIANA AND CAROL

Contents

Contents

Sugarbakers' Cookie Cutter

COOKBOOK

Introduction

My fascination with beautifully decorated, handmade cookies began 8 years ago at my daughter's school Christmas bazaar. A woman dressed like Mrs. Santa was strolling through the crowd carrying a rustic grapevine basket decorated with red and green bunting. In it were the most charming Christmas cookies I had ever seen. I picked up a 4-inch Santa, perfectly detailed right down to the cherry nose and bushy beard, the red-and-white suit, and the bag full of toys. Although the bazaar was full of Christmas crafts, none touched me like this simple cookie.

I have been a good baker since childhood and, having written three cookbooks on baking, I considered myself quite sophisticated. Yet here I was, enthralled by perfect cookie Santas, snowmen with carrot noses, and candy canes sprouting holly berries. Since the Santa cost $3.50, I decided that if I wanted to have plates and plates full of them, I should learn to make my own.

Knowing that no large corporate bakery could turn out such carefully detailed work, I set out to find my Santa's maker. My quest led me to Joy Denison, a talented designer who ran a small cottage bakery in Williams, Oregon, not far from Medford, where I live. She had been decorating for a commercial bakery, and was beginning to create and sell her own gingerbread cookies and houses.

As my interest grew, I noticed that new designs for cookie cutters, molds, and stamps were appearing on the market. Cutter shapes ranged from a heart in hand to a moose with a full rack of antlers, to such familiar cartoon characters as Mickey and Minnie Mouse. Paste dyes and edible glitters, guaranteed to awaken the artist dormant in every baker, were becoming available.

Despite these new tools for creating beautiful cookies, Joy and I soon realized that most people did not know where to start. We began developing designs for holidays and celebrations, first studying traditional cake decorating and then looking for inspiration in nature, architecture, jewelry, and fashion. We adapted our ideas to the small sizes and simple shapes of cookies, and in 1992 founded Sugarbakers' Cookies to produce our designs commercially. Now we bake and sell over 400 different cookies, but our craft remains simple and accessible to home bakers.

This collection of designs includes something for every home baker, from novice to expert. Beginners (including children) can start with sponged designs, marbled doughs, or cookie stamps. More experienced bakers will find straightforward instructions for piping simple designs with royal icing. Advanced bakers, already skilled with decorating bags, will easily master the four or five techniques used in the more complex motifs. The book also includes my favorite recipes for cookie doughs, tried and approved by my family and friends.

Baking and decorating beautiful cookies will allow you to celebrate in a very personal way your life's joyous moments—weddings, children's birthdays, and traditional holidays. Cookie decorating can also awaken your artistic instincts: I am still so fascinated by the design possibilities that my children accuse me of "seeing" cookies wherever I go. A visit to the Oregon coast inspires me to make cookies shaped like shells, crabs, and whales; after a trip to Florida, you will find me baking cookie manatees. My treasured collection of cutters grows with every trip.

Perhaps the best thing of all about the craft is its simplicity. With the talents of your eyes and hands, and a few simple tools, you can design and create cookies that will bring pleasure to you, your friends, and family. While the designs in this book encompass the festivities of a single year, the joy of decorating cookies can last a lifetime.

Equipment

*Y*our kitchen probably already contains most of the equipment you will need. Supermarkets, hardware and department stores, and low-priced warehouse shopping clubs can supply the rest.

Measuring cups: You should have one set of good-quality dry measuring cups. Metal cups are more accurate than plastic ones because they won't warp or melt in the dishwasher. If your metal cups become dented and dinged (and thus less accurate), toss them and buy new ones. You should have liquid measuring cups in 1- and 2-cup sizes. A 4-cup measure makes a nice mixing bowl for small amounts of royal icing. Corning makes clear, long-lasting, easily legible glass measures that can go into the microwave.

Measuring spoons: Choose spoons that are hooked or hinged together; individual spoons may get lost in your kitchen drawers or flour bin.

Baking sheets: Since you may use your baking sheets for sheet cakes or jelly rolls as well as cookies, buy good quality multipurpose ones. My favorite sheets are heavy-gauge aluminum; they measure 12 x 17 inches and have edges about 1 inch high.

Measure your oven before buying baking sheets: To permit adequate air flow, there should be at least 2 inches of clearance between each side of the pan and the oven wall. Purchase at least 4 sheets, so that you have a cool pair to load while another pair is in the oven. Cookies placed on a hot sheet will spread prematurely and lose their shape.

I prefer pans with a dull-to-medium shiny finish. Very shiny pans conduct heat poorly and usually have to be seasoned before use. They are difficult to maintain, requiring special plastic spatulas to preserve the finish. Black-finished pans absorb heat rapidly and may brown your cookies too quickly or burn them around the edges.

I don't have great success with those two-ply, air-filled aluminum sheets guaranteed never to burn anything: In my oven nothing browns on them in the suggested time. They may gradually take in water through the seams and leak it back unexpectedly. Although these two-ply sheets may work well for soft cookies like oatmeal raisin or chocolate chip, they're less satisfactory for the cookies in this book, which are firm and crisp.

However, if you have an older oven, two-ply sheets may be the only way to avoid burning the cookie bottoms. Make your own by stacking two thin sheets together.

Baking sheets with nonstick surfaces save time and money and work well with low-fat cookies, which hold their shape and don't spread. My favorite nonstick sheets, 10 x 15 inches, are heavy-gauge aluminum; I mail order them from Parrish Decorating Supplies or Dean & DeLuca. (See page 147 for addresses.)

Baking sheet liners: *Parchment paper liners* prevent cookies from sticking to the pan, but must be placed on cool pans before baking. Lay a sheet of parchment on the work surface, place the cut cookies on the parchment, and carefully slide the paper, cookies and all, onto the baking sheet. Since parchment liner from a roll tends to curl, keep it flat by greasing the pan lightly before transferring the first piece of paper.

Cake-decorating supply stores sell parchment by the sheet, on the roll, or in triangles precut for decorating bags. Some supermarkets sell it by the roll; some restaurant supply stores carry it in bulk at lower prices.

Aluminum foil, which has slightly more body than parchment, can also be used to line baking sheets and to transfer cut cookies from countertop to baking pan. Use foil either shiny side out or shiny side in. Lightly grease the foil if the dough is low in fat. The thin layer of foil on the baking sheet does not alter baking time.

Wire racks: As soon as your cookies are cool enough to hold their shape, transfer them from the baking sheet to a wire rack to finish cooling. You should have at least 4 racks with wires close enough together to support the cookies.

Oven: I prefer baking cookies in an electric oven because of the consistent temperature. Gas ovens tend to be more erratic. During the baking cycle oven temperatures can fluctuate at least 10° F above and below the thermostat setting, so I check the temperature with a free-standing oven thermometer.

Mixers: Any handheld electric mixer will mix the doughs in this book. Hand-held mixers demand that you pay attention, so you will never accidentally mix your dough too long or too vigorously. Both Krups and KitchenAid produce excellent models.

Sooner or later you may want a stand mixer, especially for large quantities of dough or icing. The KitchenAid K5 is excellent and, like other heavy duty mixers, comes with an all-purpose beater and a whisk, useful for royal icing. Unfortunately, stand mixers allow you to wander off while they do the beating, so unless you want to end up with tough cookies or stiff royal icing, you must pay careful attention, and shut off the machine immediately after the ingredients are thoroughly combined or the icing has reached the desired consistency.

Food processors: These high-speed machines are not ideal for making cookie dough: They can overmix in the twinkling of an eye, and the heat from the motor may warm the shortening, making the cookies flatten as they bake. On the other hand, processors are useful for chopping candies and making superfine sugar.

Rolling pins: My favorite rolling pins are long (at least 18 inches) and heavy (between 4 and 5 pounds). Constructed from hard maple, they have comfortable handles and a smooth-rolling ball-bearing system. Marble rolling pins, popular in the 1970's, remain cool and help keep dough from softening. Williams-Sonoma carries both.

A lightly floured knitted cotton sleeve slid over your rolling pin helps with soft, sticky doughs. Rubber rings that fit the ends of your pin will help produce dough of uniform thicknesses from 1/8 to 5/8 inch. The rings come in packages of 8 and are available from Yvonne's Kitchen Shoppe. (See Mail Order Sources, page 149.)

Work surfaces: Plain ordinary Formica is still my favorite surface for rolling and cutting. To enhance its nonstick properties, lightly spritz the clean surface with a fine mist of water from a spray bottle and place a sheet of plastic wrap or waxed paper on the wet surface. Lay another sheet next to it with the edges slightly overlapping. Lightly flour the wrap and you are ready to roll.

If your countertop has seams or grout, try a sheet of Sanalite, an ultrahigh-molecular-weight plastic. Flour it lightly and place a slightly damp kitchen towel on the counter to keep it from sliding around. You can order Sanalite through the mail: Munnell & Sherrill Industrial Supply (see page 147) will custom cut it (try a sheet 2 feet by 18 inches).

You may find it precut at warehouse kitchen supply stores.

To roll soft, sticky doughs (or pastry crusts), use a heavy-duty canvas pastry cloth, sprinkled and rubbed lightly with flour. The dough picks up enough flour to prevent sticking, but not enough to become tough. The cloth improves with seasoning, and need not be washed after every use. Scrape off any crumbs of dough, place it in a plastic zipper bag, and store it in the freezer, so that no little critters will make it their new home.

Instant-read thermometers: Many kitchenware stores and catalogues carry these probe-tipped thermometers, useful for checking dough temperature; chefs use them to test food as it comes from the kitchen. Standard models cost less than $15; digital ones run about $25.

Cookie cutters: Your cookie cutters are your source of inspiration, the heart and soul of your enterprise; if you don't already have a cutter collection, start one immediately. Mine began years ago when a picture of a Statue of Liberty cookie decorated with green sugar awoke me to the possibilities of baking cookies for holidays other than Christmas. Souvenir cutters have special meaning for me, as do gifts: I have a lobster cutter from friends in Maine and a manatee cutter from a Florida trip that brings back happy memories every time I use it.

You can also develop your own shapes by tracing patterns cut from cardboard about the thickness used in cereal boxes.

Commercial cutters are made from copper, plastic, or tinplate sheet steel, which produces the sharpest, thinnest, cutting edges. Tinplate and plastic cutters are inexpensive, while copper cutters, some of them handmade, can range from a fairly modest $6 to a pricey $75. The large ones make great kitchen decorations, compensating in part for their high price.

Some cutters have an enclosed back and a handle; they are more difficult to work with since you can't see the dough inside the cutter outline. You can easily cut into another cookie or leave too large a margin and have to reroll extra scraps. Rolling cutters, which have several 1- or 2-inch cutters mounted on plastic or metal rollers, can speed up the cutting process.

Wash your cutters thoroughly in warm, sudsy water after use, and dry them carefully. After baking, I place metal cutters in the still-warm oven to prevent rust from forming in the crevices around the rivets. Copper cutters won't rust, but will darken with age and discolor if water is left on them. To clean copper, apply a little ketchup with a soft cloth and let it sit until the ketchup begins to dry, 10 to 15 minutes. With extra-fine (0000 grade) steel wool, scrub off the ketchup under cool running water, and dry with a towel.

Cookie molds and stamps: Cookie molds and stamps are good to use when you are rushed: The cookies they produce require minimal decorating and are easy to make. Although cookie cutters still offer the widest choice of designs and sizes, molds and stamps are becoming increasingly available. Durable, attractive, ceramic cookie molds are useful also for molding beeswax and imprinting paper; they are sometimes available in design shops. Earthenware cookie stamps, relatively new to the market, have comfortable glazed handles and unglazed incised faces, which cut sharp patterns and release dough easily.

Brown Bag Cookie Art manufactures both molds and stamps; order them by mail from Yvonne's Kitchen Shoppe. (See Mail Order Sources, page 149.)

Pastry brushes: Use a pastry brush about an inch wide to push stuck cookies out of a cutter or to whisk excess flour from baked or unbaked cookies. A dampened brush will mend jagged edges or brush off tiny crumbs before baking. Brushes of natural bristle are the most flexible.

Decorating bags for icing: Basically, there are 2 kinds of decorating bags, store-bought and homemade. The first are made of plastic (reusable or disposable) or fabric, usually polyester. These bags can be fitted with metal decorating tips and, optionally, with couplers—devices that allow you to change tips without cleaning the icing out of the bag.

The advantage of commercially manufactured fabric or plastic bags, available in 10- and 12-inch sizes, is that they hold a lot of icing, making it easy to ice large areas or large numbers of cookies. Some are marked with a fill line, so that you don't overfill the bag and squeeze icing out the top as you begin to decorate.

Disposable plastic bags simplify cleanup; reusable bags are messy to clean but ecologically desirable. Since manufactured bags come only in fairly large sizes, they are difficult to use with small amounts of icing. Bags are available in cake-decorating supply stores and some grocery stores.

The homemade bag is a folded cone, usually of baking parchment. Some cake-decorating supply stores sell triangles of parchment ready cut for making the cones. Waxed paper will also do in a pinch, but quickly loses its crispness. Parchment cones are small, easy to handle, and simple to make. They produce neat, precise lines used with or without decorating tips. Because these parchment decorating bags are disposable and inexpensive, you can work with a number of colors at the same time. They do not work well with large amounts of icing.

White mailing envelopes make handy bags when you need only a few dots or a little outlining.

They are inexpensive and require no construction. Just snip 1/8 inch off one corner and fill with about 2 tablespoons of icing. Twist shut, and the "bag" is ready to use.

You can also use a plastic freezer zipper bag or sandwich bag, but since the plastic is soft, you will need a decorating tip and a coupler to support it.

Holders for decorating bags: Holders keep filled decorating bags upright while you are not using them. Cake decorating stores sell holders, but you can make your own inexpensively. You will need a clean sponge about 1/2-inch thick and a glass or can slightly bigger than your filled pastry bag. If you are using a can, remove one end, leaving no jagged edges. Cut the sponge to fit the can or glass; dampen the sponge and push it to the bottom of the can or glass. You can now rest the filled bag in the holder, without fear of icing dripping onto the counter or drying out in the tip.

Decorating tips and couplers: Tips are identified by numbers indicating size, and names describing the tip's family: leaf tips, writing and drawing tips, star tips, tips for rosettes, rope borders, and so on. The most prominent American manufacturers of these devices are Wilton Enterprises and Ateco; it is fortunate that both companies use the same numbering system. You can buy decorating tips individually or in handy carrying cases with as many as 50 tips to the case. I suggest buying 4 or 5 of any tip you use frequently (numbers 1, 2, and 3 round tips for example), so that you don't have to wash and reuse tips in mid-project.

The best Wilton and Ateco tips are nickel-plated and have almost invisible seams. To ensure smooth piping, check each tip before you purchase it to see that the seam is well-sealed and smooth. I do not recommend plastic tips, which lose their shape quickly and can retain grease even after washing. If you use a plastic tip for buttercream icing, you should be extraordinarily careful about reusing it with royal icing, since even a little grease in the tip can break down royal icing.

Spatulas: Once you have used an icing spatula you will never decorate cookies with a knife again. Spatulas are symmetrical, so you can use both sides of the blade for smoothing on the base coat or for decorating. You can also use a spatula to transfer cookies from counter to cookie sheet to wire rack. The most useful size has a narrow, flexible, 4-inch blade. Buy several so that you do not have to wash the same one repeatedly while you are working.

Wraps and bags: Use freezer bags, plastic produce bags, or plastic wrap to prevent dough from drying while it chills. I prefer Reynolds Plastic Wrap because it is durable. Waxed paper is ideal for layering between cookies for storage or shipping.

Ingredients

The doughs in this book are generally simple and straightforward, but if a recipe or a decorative technique calls for something esoteric, like Luster Dust, I will tell you where to find it and how to use it.

Always start with high-quality, perfectly fresh ingredients, since your cookies will only be as good as what goes into them. Nuts, citrus peel, and juice should come from this year's crop. Baking powder, eggs, and dairy products should be used before their expiration date.

For economy and convenience I reserve 1 or 2 freezer shelves for baking staples. Store flour in the freezer to prolong its freshness and keep bugs at bay. You may freeze unsalted butter for up to 4 months, but wrap it tightly or it will absorb flavors from nearby food. I buy it on sale after Halloween, in time for the holiday baking season: The price of butterfat is low then because ice cream manufacturing has decreased for winter. Purchase nuts at their peak freshness, usually in the fall, wrap them well, and freeze them to keep them from turning rancid. Buy green maraschino cherries on sale after the Christmas holidays and store them in the pantry for St. Patrick's Day.

Flour

Flours differ from one another in their protein content, which influences their behavior in the oven and the texture of the resulting product. When the proteins in flour mix with water, they form

9

gluten, which gives bread its crusty structure and strength. The more gluten (or the more it is worked and strengthened), the stronger the dough, the sturdier the texture. Too much gluten in the flour or too much handling of the dough can toughen cookies.

Unbleached all-purpose flour: Most of the recipes in this book call for unbleached all-purpose flour, which produces a texture ideal for cut and decorated cookies. Cake flour and pastry flour contain less protein, and result in cookies that are too light and soft.

Bleached all-purpose flour: Bleached all-purpose flour contains less protein than unbleached flour and will produce a softer, lighter crumb. To make softer, more delicate cookies, try substituting equal amounts of bleached flour for the unbleached all-purpose flour in the recipe. My favorite bleached flour, made by the White Lily Foods Company, is available by mail order (see page 148).

Bread flour: Bread flour is even higher in protein than unbleached all-purpose flour. Cookies baked with it will be harder, crisper, and will brown more quickly than those made with other flours. I use it for cookies that are intended as ornaments.

Soft wheat flour: Soft wheat flour is lower in protein than all-purpose flour. If you are mixing large batches in a stand mixer and find that your cookies are tough, try substituting soft wheat flour for all-purpose flour. Order by mail from the White Lily Foods Company.

Sugar

Regular granulated sugar or table sugar: The doughs in this book call for granulated sugar. It is refined from sugar beets or sugar cane.

Superfine or ultrafine sugar: Superfine sugar dissolves quickly and is used to make spun-sugar eggs and other decorations. In cookie doughs, it produces a delicate crumb.

Brown sugars: Brown sugars are ordinary refined sugars with some of the molasses from the sugar cane put back in. Dark brown sugar has 6.5 percent molasses; light brown has 3.5 percent. I prefer the dark for its pronounced flavor.

Confectioners' sugar or powdered sugar: White as snow and powdery in texture, confectioners' sugar is used to make royal icing. Because it is so fine, the manufacturer adds cornstarch to keep it from absorbing moisture from the air and clumping. I strongly recommend sifting confectioners' sugar before making royal icing to ensure that the icing will be satiny smooth and lump free. To mask the raw taste of the cornstarch, stir a small amount of fresh lemon juice or flavored extract into the icing after it has been mixed.

Decorating sugars: Decorating sugars, often dyed various colors, have a grainy appearance because their granules are about 5 times larger than those of regular granulated sugar. Buy them in cake-decorating supply stores.

Sugar crystals: Sugar crystals, less refined than decorating sugars, are available in various sizes in cake-decorating supply stores. I buy the plain crystals and dye them to my own specifications.

Eggs

All recipes have been tested using USDA grade large eggs. Eggs should stay fresh in the refrigerator for 3 to 4 weeks.

Egg whites: Raw egg whites serve as the liquid in royal icing, their albumen allowing the icing to harden. Since raw egg can be contaminated with salmonella, substitute meringue powder (see below) for raw egg whites in icing that will be eaten by babies, young children, pregnant women, or anyone with health problems.

Meringue powder: Meringue powder is egg white that has been heated, dried, and powdered. The processing kills bacteria, making meringue powder absolutely safe. It can be found in cake decorating supply stores or ordered from Yvonne's Kitchen Shoppe (see page 149).

Food Colorings

Paste dyes: These dyes, regulated by the FDA, are the most concentrated form of food coloring available and should be measured out in very small amounts, preferably on the ends of toothpicks. They are sold in 1/2-ounce containers, either individually or in kits containing up to 12 colors. Keep paste dyes tightly closed to prevent them from drying. Parrish Decorating Supplies and the New York Cake & Baking Center (see Mail Order Sources, page 147) sell larger quantities at discounted prices.

Powdered dry food coloring: Sold in jars of various sizes, this coloring is generally brushed on finished cookies to give a delicately colored sheen. Luster Dust, available from Country Kitchen Products (see Mail Order Sources, page 146) in 2-gram containers, comes in metallic colors, some with romantic names like Moonstone, Pearl Dust, and Old Gold. Be sure to order the edible varieties (the containers are clearly labeled), which are FDA approved. I brush it on dry or dilute it with a little lemon extract to paint over decorated cookies. Christmas cookies finished with Luster Dust will acquire the soft glow of traditional Old World ornaments.

Fats

Cookies need fat to bind the dry ingredients, to impart tenderness, and to give flavor. The kind and amount of fat you choose influences the shape and texture of your cookies.

Unsalted sweet butter: With its rich, sweet taste, unsalted butter is especially good to use in cookies decorated with bland-tasting royal icing. However, butter is sensitive to temperature, which can make it tricky to work with; it is almost rock hard in the refrigerator, but becomes soft and spreadable at room temperature and melts completely at about 90° F.

Vegetable shortening: Vegetable shortening is good for rolled and cut cookies because it remains solid, though soft and malleable, over a broad temperature range. It is less likely than butter to seep through royal icing and make the colors bleed. Cookies made with shortening tolerate varying storage temperatures and do not spoil as quickly as butter cookies.

Cream: The recipes in this book call for heavy or whipping cream. Store it at the back of your refrigerator (the coldest part) to maintain freshness.

Chocolate

Unsweetened cocoa powder: Cocoa powder, made from ground cocoa beans with three-fourths of the cocoa butter removed, is my favorite form of chocolate for cookie doughs. Cookies made with it stay crisp and hold their shape better than cookies made using solid chocolate, which has a higher fat content.

Unsweetened cocoa powder comes in 2 forms. Natural cocoa, which is less expensive, results from grinding the beans, extracting fat, and grinding again. Dutched cocoa has been treated with an alkali to reduce bitterness, darken the color, and mellow the flavor. I prefer Dutch-process cocoa, but you can substitute natural cocoa in equal amounts. Some brands are more intensely flavored and colored than others, so experiment to find one you like. I recommend Pernigotti, an Italian cocoa carried by Williams-Sonoma, and Guittard's, available in cake-baking and decorating-supply stores.

Spices, Extracts, and Essences

Spices: Buy spices in small quantities, if possible in their natural form (cinnamon sticks, whole nutmeg seeds, allspice berries, and vanilla beans), and grind them yourself to give your cookies a sublime flavor. I grate nutmeg on a small nutmeg grater, but grind cinnamon sticks, broken into small pieces, in a coffee grinder that I reserve for that purpose. Store spices in air-tight containers in a cool, dark place.

Almond and lemon extracts: Almond and lemon extracts enhance the flavor of cookies that contain those ingredients. Don't buy imitation flavorings; pure extracts, though more expensive, have more intense flavor. Avoid tinted extracts if you do not want them to discolor white batter or royal icing.

Vanilla extract: Pure vanilla extract is expensive. Since my children and husband put it in everything, including pancake batter, I buy it in quantity, preferably on sale or at my warehouse shopping club. Rose Beranbaum, author of *The Cake Bible,* suggests storing liquid extract in a squeeze bottle and intensifying the flavor by submerging a vanilla bean in it.

Essences: True essences are highly concentrated flavorings distilled from natural ingredients. Flavors include mandarin orange, lime, pineapple, and even cocoa for chocolate doughs. Essences are sold in very small quantities and measured by the drop. Never pour an essence directly into the mixing bowl, since even one extra drop may be too much! I stir essence into icing a single drop a time, until I get the flavor intensity I want. Orange flower water or rose water, which are less concentrated, can be used more freely.

Dragées

Dragées (pronounced with a soft "g"), shiny little silver and gold balls made mostly of sugar, have been accepted by the USDA for use as food decoration. They are nontoxic in small quantities, but you should not eat them by the spoonful, handful, or bowlful. You can buy dragées in cake-decorating supply stores; the New York Cake & Baking Center (see Mail Order Sources, page 147) carries them in several sizes and in pastel colors as well as silver and gold.

Molasses

Unsulfured molasses tastes better than the sulphured variety and works well in gingerbread and spice doughs. To measure, lightly grease a liquid measuring cup before adding the molasses; it will pour out without leaving a thick coating behind.

Nuts

Pecans, black walnuts, English walnuts, almonds, and pistachios are all fine additions to cookie dough. Salted nuts cut the sweetness of doughs and icings, but if you don't want the extra sodium, place the nuts in a strainer and rinse with hot water. Thoroughly dry them in a towel before grinding.

Black walnuts, very popular in the 1950's, are still among my favorites. They are delicious in banana breads and cakes, and wonderful minced and added to any butter cookie. Because they are difficult to shell, I buy them already hulled from Harry and David's mail-order catalogue (see Mail Order Sources, page 147).

Hazelnuts and some other nuts have bitter skins. To remove the peels, bake the nuts in a 350° F oven for 10 minutes; then place them in a thick, rough towel. Wrap the towel around them completely and let them steam for 5 minutes. Then rub off as much skin as you can with the towel.

Alternatively, blanch the nuts for 3 minutes in boiling water to which a touch of baking soda has been added. Drain the nuts and slip off the peels. Crisp them in a 350° F oven for 10 minutes. Cool before grinding or chopping.

Lightly toasting nuts brings their oil to the surface and strengthens flavor, but can overpower the taste of other ingredients. If you are making delicately flavored cookies like shortbread, skip the toasting unless you want a robust, nutty flavor.

Citrus Zest

The zest is the colored portion of the peel of lemons, oranges, limes, or grapefruit. Added to shortbread or sugar cookies, zest imparts a sweet yet tangy quality without overpowering other flavors. Since citrus fruits are usually waxed and may have traces of pesticides, wash the fruit carefully and scrub it with extra-fine (0000) steel wool before removing the zest. If you are going to use the juice, roll the fruit on the countertop using light pressure; then heat the fruit in the microwave for 10 to 15 seconds before you remove the zest. This procedure helps in extracting as much juice as possible.

Remove the zest, shaving off only the colored part of the rind and leaving the bitter white pith. I use a citrus zester, which produces thin strings of zest. Mince the zest or put it in the food processor along with the sugar required by the recipe. The processor disperses the zest nicely and guarantees that it will be well-combined with the other ingredients. Peel or squeeze the fruit after you have removed the zest.

CHAPTER 3

A Word to the Wise Baker:

Tips for Cookie Baking Success

Before You Bake

Several hours or even the day before you bake, read your recipe carefully. Make sure you have all ingredients, supplies (including parchment paper), and equipment (including mixer attachments) at the ready, so you don't have to dash to the store or rummage through your cabinets at some critical point. Grease or paper your pans before you get your hands messy. Preheat the oven.

Mixing the Dough

Measure all ingredients accurately. For flour and white sugar, use a measuring cup with a smooth, even rim. Dip the cup into the flour or sugar

bin and level with a flat-edged knife or spatula. Don't pack the flour into the cup or use a liquid measure with a raised lip: You can mistakenly measure out too much. Do pack brown sugar into the measuring cup with the back of a spoon. Measure liquids in a transparent glass measure resting on a level surface. Lower your eyes to cup level and check for accuracy.

If necessary, adjust the amount of liquid to achieve the correct texture. If the dough doesn't easily come together to form a pliable mass, knead in extra dribbles of milk or water. This makes the dough easier to roll out and minimizes cracking around the edges. If the dough seems sticky, refrigerate it for at least 30 minutes or add a little more flour.

To make butter workable, bring it to room temperature. Leave it on the kitchen counter for 30 minutes to an hour (depending on the temperature of your kitchen), or soften it quickly in your microwave. Place 1 or 2 sticks in the microwave and cook on high for 5 seconds. Squeeze the sticks; if they are still firm, roll them a quarter turn and heat again. Continue heating and turning at 5-second intervals, until the butter gives a little.

Rolling and Cutting the Cookies

If your dough is sticky, wrap it in plastic and refrigerate for about 30 minutes. Dough at 72° F is ideal for rolling—pliable, cool, and nonsticky. Use an instant-read food thermometer to check the temperature.

Chilled dough rolls best if it has been refrigerated no longer than 3 hours. If it has gotten too cold, let it sit for 30 minutes at room temperature. In an emergency you can soften hard (not frozen) dough in the microwave, but be careful since the microwave can suddenly turn it into a sticky mess. In a 750-watt microwave, warm the dough on high for less than 5 seconds; rotate it and turn it over; test the consistency. Repeat if necessary. Fifteen seconds in all should be adequate. With a more powerful microwave, reduce the power level before heating the dough; it is always easier to repeat the procedure than to firm up sticky dough. The dough is ready when it is pliable when pinched but still cool to the touch.

Use a light hand flouring the work surface and rolling pin otherwise the dough will absorb excess flour, toughening the cookies. If you work on Formica or Sanalite, overflouring will seldom cause you problems.

To make delicate cookies or cookie sandwiches, roll the dough thin about 1/4 inch. For shortbreads or sturdy ornaments, leave the dough as thick as 3/8 inch.

Cut out a test cookie; if it sticks, flour the cutter, shake off the excess, and try again. Push the cutter firmly into the dough, pressing evenly around the entire edge to make sure that the dough is completely cut. This is especially important when working with large cutters or doughs that contain fruit or nuts. Reflour the cutter as needed. You may also trace a thin cardboard pattern using a sharp knife. Cut the cookies close together to minimize scraps.

If a cookie doesn't fall easily from the cutter, gently push a pastry brush against the stuck edge. You can also use the pastry brush to smooth rough edges or whisk away excess flour and crumbs.

Gather and reroll the scraps; cut again. If the dough has warmed, you may have to rewrap and refrigerate it briefly before rerolling and cutting. The extra handling will make rerolled cookies a little tougher than the first batch.

Putting the Cookies on Baking Sheets

Line baking sheets with parchment paper or grease them with vegetable shortening, spreading on a thin film with a clean rag or wad of plastic wrap. You may use unsalted butter, but apply it sparingly, since too much butter makes the cookies soften, spread, or burn around the edges. I don't recommend nonstick vegetable sprays which sometimes bake onto the pan, forming a sticky yellow residue that requires steel wool and elbow grease to remove.

Transfer cookies to the baking sheet using a flexible spatula wide enough to support the entire cookie. Lay them out evenly, keeping them at least an inch apart. Soft cookies (like sugar cookies) generally puff and spread more than firm, thick cookies (like gingerbread cookies).

If you don't have enough sheets to hold a whole batch at once, you will have to work in stages, cooling the pans completely before reloading them: Hot baking sheets cause raw cookies to spread prematurely and lose their shape. You may cool high-quality baking sheets by running them under cold water and drying them immediately, but the shock of the cold water may warp inexpensive sheets.

Since cookies cut from high-fat dough may stick to the work surface (especially in a warm kitchen), you should refrigerate the uncut dough while the first sheets are baking; cut the next batch just before loading the sheets. If you don't have time for this, cut out all the cookies, place them on sheets of foil or parchment, and store them flat on a cleared shelf in the refrigerator.

If, however, your kitchen is cool and the waiting time is brief, place the cookies on parchment or foil, leave them on the counter, and transfer them to the baking pans as soon as possible. If you have used foil, you don't have to cool the baking pans, but you must put the loaded sheet into the oven immediately. If you have used parchment, you must cool the pan.

Always preheat the oven for at least 15 minutes. The initial blast of heat sets the cookies so that they don't spread and burn around the edges. If you don't preheat the oven, the fat in the dough will begin to melt as the temperature rises, and the cookies will flatten out.

Cookies bake best in the middle of the oven. If the oven rack is too high, the cookies may brown too much. If it is too low, the bottoms may burn. You can bake 2 sheets of cookies simultaneously if you are very careful: Arrange the racks to divide the oven into thirds and, halfway through the baking time, rotate the pans from top to bottom and from front to back. Use this technique only when you are truly rushed, and watch the cookies closely.

Stamping and Molding Cookies

Stamped or molded cookies are easy to make and don't require a floured work surface, an advantage when baking with children, who can easily turn your kitchen into a floury shambles.

To stamp cookies, chill the dough and form into 2-inch balls. Place the balls on a parchment-lined baking sheet, flatten to about 1/2-inch with your hand or the back of a nonstick pancake turner. Then simply stamp and bake.

To make molded cookies, spray the mold with a very light coating of nonstick vegetable oil. Lightly flour the mold and tap it on the countertop to remove excess. Press chilled cookie dough into the mold until it is completely full. Invert the mold and tap the edge on the countertop, rotating between taps, until the cookie falls out. Reflour but do not regrease the mold and repeat the procedure.

Place the cookies on baking sheets and bake in the upper third of the oven. This helps them to brown nicely, highlighting the detail of the relief.

Common Cookie Problems and Their Solutions

My cookie dough is too soft or sticky to roll.

Causes: The dough is either too warm or contains too much liquid.

Solutions: Cover it with plastic wrap and refrigerate until firm enough to handle. Or, work with a small part of the dough, refrigerating the rest until ready to use. If the dough is sticky even when cold, lightly flour both the work surface and the dough before rolling and cutting.

The cookies run into each other while baking.

Causes: The cookies were placed too close together on the baking sheet or the dough contained too much leavening, making the cookies rise and spread excessively.

Solutions: Remember to space cookies at least 1 to 2 inches apart on the baking sheet. Measure baking powder and baking soda accurately, using standardized measuring spoons.

The cookies spread and thin out while baking.

Causes: The baking sheet was greased too heavily, or was hot when you loaded it. The cut cookies were too warm when you put them on the sheet.

Solutions: Grease the baking sheets with a thin, even layer of shortening, never liquid vegetable oil. Bake your cookies immediately after placing them on sheets or store the loaded sheets in the refrigerator until ready to bake. Cool the baking sheets between batches.

The dough is crumbly and dry; it cracks excessively around the edges when rolled.

Causes: The dough may contain too little liquid or shortening, or too much flour. The dough is too cold.

Solutions: Measure all liquids accurately in a glass liquid measure; the recipes in this book call for large eggs. Add 1 or 2 tablespoons of milk or water to the dough and mix thoroughly to incorporate. Measure flour accurately, using the dip and sweep method; be sure you level the measure with a flat knife blade. Let the dough sit at room temperature for an additional 15 minutes.

The cookies are too crisp and too dark on the bottom.

Causes: The oven was too hot. The cookies were placed in the oven before it had completely preheated. The baking sheet was too dark or too thin. The cookies were baked too low in the oven. The baking sheets were overgreased.

Solutions: Check oven calibration with an independent thermometer. Preheat the oven for at least 15 minutes. Use shiny, heavy-gauge aluminum baking sheets. Stack 2 thin baking sheets together or try commercial two-ply aluminum sheets. Bake on the middle shelf. Grease the baking sheet with a thin, even layer of shortening, not vegetable oil.

The cookies are too dry or too moist.

Causes: Overbaking or underbaking.

Solutions: To prevent overbaking, check the cookies 1 or 2 minutes before the minimum baking time has elapsed. If they are not done, reset the timer and bake a few minutes longer, checking at 1- to 2-minute intervals by lightly depressing the middle of a cookie with your finger. It is done when it springs back immediately.

The cookies crack and fall apart as they're removed from the baking sheet.

Causes: Some higher fat cookies are fragile when hot.

Solutions: Allow cookies to cool on the baking sheets for 2 or 3 minutes before removing them to a rack. Use a flexible pancake turner large enough to support the entire cookie.

The cookies stick to the baking sheet.

Causes: The baking sheet was inadequately prepared. The cookies cooled too long on the baking sheet.

Solutions: Grease the baking sheet evenly or cover it with parchment paper. To unstick cookies, return them to the oven for 1 or 2 minutes and then immediately remove them from the baking sheet to a rack.

The sheet of cookies bakes unevenly.

Causes: The cookies were not rolled to a uniform thickness or cut with the same cutter. The oven has hot spots.

Solutions: If possible, load each baking sheet with cookies of the same size and thickness. Reverse the sheets from front to back halfway through the baking period. If baking 2 sheets at a time, also rotate them from top to bottom.

Molded cookies stick to the mold.

Causes: The mold was prepared with too much fat and not enough flour.

Solutions: Spritz the molds lightly with nonstick vegetable-oil spray and then flour them. Rap the mold on the countertop to knock out all excess flour before adding dough.

Molded or stamped cookies lose detail while baking.

Causes: The dough contained too much leavening, causing the cookie to rise too much and lose detail. The dough was not molded or stamped with enough force to pick up the detail. The cookies were not baked immediately after being shaped.

Solutions: Choose a recipe with minimal baking powder or baking soda. Pack the cookie mold crevices and crannies completely so that the cookie will be fully detailed. Stamp cookies with enough force to imprint the surface strongly. Don't allow unbaked cookies to sit longer than 10 minutes before baking.

Storing Dough and Cookies

For ornaments or cookies that must keep, choose a dough lower in fat than that for cookies you will eat immediately. The fat in rich cookies can leak through the icing and make the colors bleed. Butter is a worse culprit than vegetable shortening, so eat buttery cookies within a week (not usually a hardship!).

Dough: Most cookie doughs can be successfully refrigerated for up to 1 week. Use plastic containers with tight-fitting lids, or put the dough in a reclosable plastic bag and press out excess air. Dough can be frozen for several weeks. Thaw it overnight in the refrigerator.

Undecorated baked cookies: If you want to work on a major baking job a little at a time, you can bake your cookies, freeze them for several months, and decorate them later. Undecorated cookies last better in the freezer if they are cut fairly thick ($1/4$- to $3/8$-inch) and baked crisp. Place the cookies in heavy-duty reclosable freezer bags, expelling excess air. Pack the bags into rigid containers so the cookies won't get crushed in the freezer. Flash-freeze thin cookies: Put them in single layers onto cookie sheets and freeze in the coldest part of the freezer. When frozen solid, pack them into plastic bags and put the bags into crushproof containers.

Decorated baked cookies: Do not freeze cookies decorated with royal icing, which will separate from the cookie base when frozen. You can freeze cookies decorated with other icings for 3 to 6 months.

Decorated cookies made with low-fat dough will keep for several months at room temperature if stored in tins or lidded glass jars and put in a cool dark place; light, particularly fluorescent light, will fade the icing. Make sure the icing is thoroughly dry before storing.

Crisp cookies: Do not store for long periods at room temperature in tightly closed plastic containers; the moisture in the cookies creates a "greenhouse effect" and eventually softens the crispness.

For shorter periods, lidded plastic containers, reclosable plastic bags, or ceramic cookie jars are fine for both crisp and soft cookies. Layer the cookies between paper towels or sheets of waxed paper. The paper towels provide extra cushioning for designs with raised borders or delicate flower tips or buds.

Shipping Cookies

Cookies that freeze well will ship well. Make them with low-fat dough, cut them $3/8$- to $1/2$-inch thick, and bake them until crisp: chances are they will survive their journey unbroken. Dry the cookies for 18–24 hours after you decorate them, before wrapping and shipping.

At Sugarbakers' we shrink-wrap each cookie before shipping, but you can substitute ordinary plastic wrap. The Reynolds Aluminum Company manufactures it in colors suitable for different holidays. For large cookies, twist the wrap around individual cookies and tie off at the top. Pack the cookies into cellophane or decorative paper bags (card shops sell them); top off the bags with ribbon. Wrap medium or small cookies individually with plastic and place in egg cartons or clean, lidded yogurt containers. You can also layer squares of waxed paper between individual cookies to keep them from rubbing against one another.

Choose a shipping box of heavy corrugated cardboard. Line the bottom with a 2-inch layer of styrofoam peanuts, bubble wrap, or other lightweight packing material. Pack the yogurt containers, egg cartons, or bags of wrapped cookies in the carton. Pad the sides and top with at least 2 inches of ink-free newsprint, bubble wrap, or styrofoam. The cookies and packing material should be packed so tightly that nothing moves or rattles when you shake the package.

The Icing on the Cookie:

Techniques for Making and Decorating with Icing

Thinking about Design and Color

Tinted icing, colored sugars, dragées, and sugar beads can transform plain, ordinary cookies into edible works of art. But remember that in baking as well as in architecture, less is often more; if you are going to err, do so on the side of understatement.

Let the shape of the cutter guide your major decisions. Lip-shaped Valentine cookies need only a coating of kiss-me-dead red icing to convey their message. A dachshund cutter with short legs and a skinny body instantly suggests dogginess. Choose dark dough and brown icing to complement it; use a black outline to disguise ragged edges and acci-

dental drips. Add toenails, eyes, and other simple details for style.

When planning my icing colors, I use a color wheel. Pastels and light hues generally look more attractive on cookies than dark colors, so I usually choose a tone from the rim of the wheel where the hues are less intense. It's easier to intensify a hue with food coloring than to soften it with white icing. Complementary colors, directly opposite one another on the wheel, may suggest certain traditional holiday combinations, especially red and green, and purple and yellow. Start with them, or experiment until your own combination looks right.

Try to match the dough color to the intensity of the icing. For Halloween choose chocolate, gin-

Royal Icing with Egg Whites—1 Pound (3 cups)

OUTLINE CONSISTENCY	BASE CONSISTENCY	FLOW CONSISTENCY
3 $^3/_4$ cups confectioners' sugar	3 $^3/_4$ cups confectioners' sugar	3 $^3/_4$ cups confectioners' sugar
3 large egg whites	3 large egg whites	3 large egg whites
$^1/_2$ teaspoon cream of tartar	$^1/_2$ teaspoon cream of tartar	$^1/_2$ teaspoon cream of tartar
$^1/_2$ teaspoon lemon extract, optional	$^1/_2$ teaspoon lemon extract, optional	$^1/_2$ teaspoon lemon extract, optional
no extra water	1 tablespoon water	2 tablespoons water
Beat 6—8 minutes	Beat 6—8 minutes	Beat 6—8 minutes

gerbread, or spice dough to stand up to the assertive browns, blacks, and oranges of the decoration and to hide any bleeding that may occur with these intense, rich colors. For Easter or Valentine's Day choose a shortbread or a sugar cookie to enhance pale pinks and yellows.

Before you bake, work out your design with colored pencils, outlining your cutter on white or brown paper, depending on the dough you choose. When the background colors please you, add outlines and other decorative details.

Royal Icing

Royal icing, which hardens to a glossy, alabaster finish, is ideal for decorating cookies. In its purest form, it contains only 3 ingredients: confectioners' sugar, water, and raw egg white or meringue powder. Thinned with water, it spreads easily and flattens as it dries to make a smooth background. Mixed thickly, it can be used for piped decorations like rosettes. It is durable and stands up well to handling and shipping.

The main drawback of royal icing is that it can taste like cornstarch, which is added to confectioners' sugar to prevent clumping. I disguise this starchiness with flavorful extracts, essences, or oils. I also occasionally add flavorings to mask the taste of food coloring, sometimes noticeable when large amounts are needed for dark or jewel tones. Now coming onto the market are paste dyes labeled "tasteless" or "taste-free," which have no discernible dye flavor; look for them, especially if you are working with red or black. For extra-shiny icing, add a few drops of glycerin, available at drug stores. Since royal icing lacks the smooth richness of

Royal Icing with Meringue Powder

Outline Consistency

FOR ¹/₂ POUND (1 ¹/₂ CUPS) ICING	**FOR 1 POUND (3 CUPS) ICING**	**FOR 2 POUNDS (6 CUPS) ICING**
2 cups confectioners' sugar	3 ³/₄ cups confectioners' sugar	7 ¹/₂ cups confectioners' sugar
1 tablespoon + 1 teaspoon meringue powder	3 tablespoons meringue powder	¹/₄ cup + 2 tablespoons meringue powder
3 tablespoons + 1 teaspoon warm water	6 tablespoons warm water	³/₄ cup warm water
Beat 3–5 mins	Beat 4–5 mins	Beat 6–8 mins

butter or cream, it tastes best on cookies with a high fat content.

Getting Started with Royal Icing

1. Organize before you begin. Plan your design; select your dyes. Lay out ingredients and utensils; assemble decorating bags.

2. If you are unfamiliar with royal icing, experiment with a practice batch until you get some feel for handling different consistencies.

3. Make sure your utensils and bowl are absolutely clean and free of grease; otherwise, the icing won't peak properly.

4. Sift confectioners' sugar before mixing icing.

5. Separate eggs carefully. An egg at room temperature separates more easily than one straight from the refrigerator. Gently crack the egg on a bowl rim or with the dull edge of a knife. Holding the egg over the bowl, carefully tear the shell in two. Slowly pour the contents back and forth from one shell into the other, letting the white dribble into the bowl while keeping the yolk intact.

6. Take care not to overbeat royal icing, especially if you are using a stand mixer; 6–8 minutes will suffice for 6 cups of icing. Overbeaten icing will stiffen and become opaque and dry, making it difficult to work with and impos-

Royal Icing with Meringue Powder

Base Consistency

FOR ½ POUND (1½ CUPS) ICING	FOR 1 POUND (3 CUPS) ICING	FOR 2 POUNDS (6 CUPS) ICING
2 cups confectioners' sugar	3 ¾ cups confectioners' sugar	7 ½ cups confectioners' sugar
1 tablespoon + 1 teaspoon meringue powder	3 tablespoons meringue powder	¼ cup + 2 tablespoons meringue powder
4 tablespoons warm water	7 tablespoons warm water	¾ cup + 1 tablespoon warm water
Beat 3–5 mins	Beat 4–5 mins	Beat 6–8 mins

sible to pipe through a small tip. Use over-beaten icing for rosettes, borders, or other decorations that require a #3 (or larger) tip. Make a fresh batch for base coating or delicate designs.

7. If you plan to flavor the icing, choose a flavor compatible with your cookies—root beer or bubble gum for children's cookies, lemon and orange for citrus shortbreads or sugar cookies. Add flavored oils drop by drop, tasting after each addition.

8. Don't leave royal icing uncovered. Cover the container with a tight lid, damp cloth, or plastic wrap. Although I prefer making icing one batch at a time and using it immediately, royal icing will last about a week in the refrigerator or about a month in the freezer. If necessary, thin with spoonfuls of water into which you have whisked a little meringue powder.

Recipes for Royal Icing

Royal icing can be made with meringue powder or with raw eggs. Since raw egg can contain salmonella, it should not be used in food for pregnant women, babies, small children, or anyone with health problems. To be absolutely safe, choose a recipe with meringue powder.

You will need 3 basic consistencies for the designs in this book: *outline consistency* for firm curved or straight lines and handwritten script; *base consistency,* for flat base coatings, raised dots, flowers, and soft lines; and *flow consistency,* for filling in outlines, or for flat dots that melt into a

Royal Icing with Meringue Powder

Flow Consistency

FOR ½ POUND (1½ CUPS) ICING	FOR 1 POUND (3 CUPS) ICING	FOR 2 POUNDS (6 CUPS) ICING
2 cups confectioners' sugar	3 ¾ cups confectioners' sugar	7 ½ cups confectioners' sugar
1 tablespoon + 1 teaspoon meringue powder	3 tablespoons meringue powder	¼ cup + 2 tablespoons meringue powder
5 tablespoons warm water	8 tablespoons warm water	1 cup warm water
Beat 3–5 mins	Beat 4–5 mins	Beat 6–8 mins

background. The preceding tables, with recipes containing either raw egg whites or meringue powder, give proportions and beating times for these consistencies.

Making the Icing

Making royal icing couldn't be easier. The consistency will depend on the amount of water and the length of beating time.

1. If the recipe calls for meringue powder, briefly mix the powder and sugar together with a hand-held electric mixer before adding the water; this ensures lump-free icing. Then add the water and beat at slow speed until the icing reaches desired consistency.

2. If the recipe calls for egg whites, simply beat together the sugar, egg whites, and cream of tartar until the icing reaches desired consistency.

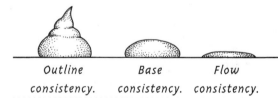

Outline consistency.   Base consistency.   Flow consistency.

3. Test the icing for consistency.

FOR OUTLINE ICING: Put 1 teaspoon of icing into the decorating tip you will use. With your finger, gently push the icing through the tip onto a piece of waxed paper. If the icing on the paper seems wet and runny, add sugar, 1 tablespoon at a time, and beat on low until thoroughly blended; do not overbeat. If the icing remaining on the tip curls back, like an elephant's raised trunk, the icing is too dry. Stir in dribbles of water with a spoon (the mixer might introduce air bubbles) until the icing reaches the desired consistency.

FOR BASE ICING: Cover approximately one-third of the base area of a test cookie with icing. Begin in the middle, and, holding the cookie in your hand, push the icing with a spatula to the edge of the cookie, smoothing as you go. If the icing drips or runs off the edge, thicken the batch with more confectioners' sugar. The icing should spread smoothly, not sticking to the underside of the spatula or making rough streaks; light streaks will disappear as more icing is added and begins to set.

FOR FLOW ICING: With a teaspoon, pour a little icing onto a small cookie with icing outlines already in place; the flow icing should take 3 to 4 seconds to settle and flow to the edges. If it runs immediately, it is too thin. Add sifted confectioners' sugar a teaspoonful at a time and whisk thoroughly until you reach the right consistency. Don't thin the icing too much or it will lose its sheen. The icing should flow easily when stirred with a spoon but retain a hint of body.

4. By hand, stir in optional flavorings.

5. Place the icing in clean containers, one for each different color to be used. Tint according to directions on pages 31–32. Cover tightly until ready to fill the decorating bag.

After you tint the icing, you may have to change the consistency to achieve different effects with the same color. While you are decorating, the consistency may change as the icing stands, and you may have to fine tune it. To thicken the icing, add more confectioners' sugar. To thin the icing, add warm water mixed with meringue powder: Use 1 tablespoon of powder per 1/2 cup water. The meringue powder will keep the icing from losing its body.

Recipes for Other Icings

Buttercream Icing

Buttercream icing, richer than royal icing, has more body and lift. I use it for raised designs including ribbons, roses, and other flowers. Although buttercream will firm up if allowed to sit for 24 hours, it will never become as hard as royal icing, and is thus not recommended for cookies that will be stacked or shipped.

3 tablespoons butter at room temperature	2 tablespoons milk
3 tablespoons vegetable shortening	1/2 teaspoon vanilla extract
1 1/2 cups confectioners' sugar	Paste food coloring, optional

In a medium mixing bowl, beat together the butter, shortening, sugar, milk, and vanilla extract until thoroughly combined and velvety smooth. Tint with paste dye if desired.

Makes approximately 1 cup of icing.

Corn Syrup Glaze

*T*his glaze will completely coat the top and sides of a cookie. Left untinted, it remains transparent and looks attractive poured over flattened edible flowers for Wedding Cookies or Victorian Valentines; it also works well on petits fours.

¹/₂ cup water	2 ¹/₂ teaspoons almond extract
¹/₄ cup light corn syrup	4 to 6 teaspoons half-and-half
8 cups sifted confectioners' sugar	Paste food coloring, optional

1. Put the water and corn syrup in a large, heavy saucepan. Add the sugar, and stir until thoroughly combined.

2. Using a wet pastry brush, wash down any sugar crystals on the sides of the pan.

3. Attach a candy thermometer to the side of the pan, making sure it does not touch the bottom. Heat over medium-low heat, stirring constantly until the icing reaches 100° F. Remove from heat.

4. Stir in almond extract and 4 teaspoons half-and-half. Cool the icing for 5 minutes. Use additional half-and-half to thin to the consistency of corn syrup. Tint with paste dyes if desired.

5. Place cookies on a rack set over a baking sheet with 1-inch raised sides. Slowly pour the glaze over the cookies, completely coating them. Let dry until glaze begins to harden and crust over. Decorate with additional royal icing as desired.

Clearly Vanilla Icing

Vegetable shortening and clear vanilla extract combine with confectioners' sugar to make an exceptionally white and slightly fluffy icing. It is easy to make and softer than royal icing, but will harden if left to dry for at least 24 hours. Clear vanilla extract is available in cake-decorating supply stores or by mail order.

3 cups confectioners' sugar	5 to 6 tablespoons skim milk
6 tablespoons vegetable shortening	Paste food colorings, optional
3/4 teaspoon clear vanilla extract	

In a medium bowl combine the sugar, shortening, vanilla extract, and 5 tablespoons milk. Beat with an electric mixer until smooth. Add the additional tablespoon of milk, if needed, to reach a consistency that will pipe well and hold its shape instantly. Tint with paste food colorings if desired.

Cookie Crumbs

Glaze that drips onto the cookie sheet can be used again if crumb-free. If it has cooled and crusted, scrape it into a container and warm in the microwave for about 15 seconds. Whisk until it pours easily.

Coloring the Icing

1. Before you tint a batch of white icing, decide how many colors you will need and estimate the amount of icing for each color. Divide the icing into separate containers. To add paste or dry powder colors to royal icing, dip a toothpick into the dye. Transfer the color to the icing, and stir with a spoon until no streaks of dye remain. Use a clean toothpick to add more coloring.

Since colors may intensify as they sit, stop while the icing is slightly paler than desired and let it rest 15–30 minutes. If the color doesn't intensify, continue adding dye until you reach the desired shade.

2. Make notes on colors that were difficult to create or especially successful: Record the amount of white icing, the brand and color of the dye, the number of toothpickfuls of dye. Take a color photo of the icing or decorated cookie.

3. Before adding lines or decorations of contrasting colors adjacent to the outlines, let outlines dry until crusted. Before filling adjacent areas with contrasting flow icing, let outlines dry at least 2 hours.

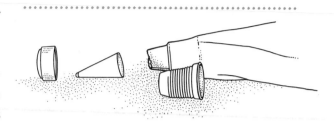

Coupler ring, tip, bag, and coupler base.

Working with Decorating Bags

Preparing a Plastic or Cloth Decorating Bag

To install a metal decorating tip in a purchased bag, simply drop the tip into the bag and push it down as far as it will go. It should protrude about ¹/₂ inch through the hole at the end of the bag; if it does not, remove it and trim the end of the bag ¹/₈ inch at a time, enlarging the hole until the tip fits properly.

If you plan to change tips while using the same color icing, you should install a *coupler,* a 2-part plastic device that fits into the tip of the bag. The 2 parts are a conical base and a small ring that looks like an old-fashioned baby-bottle top without the nipple. The 2 pieces are threaded so they can be screwed together. A coupler will also prevent a small tip from working itself back into the bag as you decorate.

To install the coupler, drop the base into the bag, narrow end down. Push it down as far as it will go. Use a pencil to mark the place on the outside of the bag where the coupler's last thread makes a groove against the fabric of the bag. Take out the coupler base and trim the bag at the pencil line.

Insert the coupler base again. Make sure that 1 or 2 threads protrude through the hole in the bag. Place the metal decorating tip over the coupler base and then screw the ring onto the base. When you want to change tips, simply unscrew the ring.

Filling the Bag

Hold the bag in the middle and fold the top down several inches on the outside, like a wide cuff. Fill the bag half way; don't overfill or icing will squeeze out the top when you close it. Unfold the cuff and gently force the icing down into the bag, kneading out any air pockets. Firmly twist the empty top of the bag until it is securely closed.

To keep the bag shut when you lay it on the table, twist a metal or plastic twist tie around the open end. Zip plastic sandwich or freezer bags closed.

Constructing and Filling a Parchment Cone

For small amounts of icing, you can make your own icing cones. Cut out a square of parchment paper 8 inches long on each side. Fold the paper in half diagonally. Cut it along the diagonal edge. This will give you 2 triangles. Their short sides will be 8 inches. The long side will be just a shade longer than 11 inches. You will need only 1 triangle for each cone.

Label the points A, B, and C. Label the middle of the long side X. (See figures on page 34.)

Put point A at the top. If you are right-handed, pick up point B. Curl point B up and under, giving it a half twist. Continue curling until the back of Point B rests against the front of point A. The mouth of the cone will be made of the edge between A and B. The point of the cone will be at X.

Now pick up the other point, point C. Wrap it around the outside of the cone until it meets points B and A behind the cone. If you look at the cone with the opening facing you, B will be closest to you, A will be under it, and C will be under A.

Adjust the cone so that the point is absolutely sharp and completely closed; tugging gently on points B and C might help. Fold the 3 points A, B, and C, down into the cone to even out the top. Tape or staple them together if you wish.

Tape the long seam shut from the mouth of the cone all the way down to the point. Strengthen the cone by putting tape around it near the point; this will help keep icing from leaking out the seam when you squeeze.

If you plan to use a metal tip, it is probably better to use a coupler also, unless you are working with a very small amount of icing in a very short time; otherwise the cone can leak and the procedure become very messy. If you wish to use the parchment cone without a metal tip to pipe a very thin line of icing, snip off about $1/16$ inch of the paper. Cut off more of the cone for a wider line of piping. Cut about $3/4$ inch from the point of the cone and drop in a coupler. Push it down for a snug fit. Screw the tip onto the coupler.

Fill the bag about half full. Fold down the top 2 or 3 times. As you squeeze out icing, continue to fold down the top.

Basic Procedures for Decorating

Decorating can be a messy business, so it is good to have an operating plan when you begin. Mix the master recipe of icing to the thickest consistency you will need for your design. Divide the icing into small bowls, one for each color. Tint each bowl of icing to the desired hue and dilute (if necessary) to the desired consistency. If different shades or consistencies of a single color are required, divide that color into smaller batches and dilute or tint as needed. Keep icing covered when you are not actually using it.

Method One: Working from the Base Up

Cookies decorated this way are built like houses, starting at ground level. The technique creates a smooth background of base icing that covers the entire cookie; decorative details are piped on top. The golden leaves (photo 4) were made by this method.

1. Choose background and decorative colors. Mix and tint all the trim and special piping colors first. Then mix the base color with the remaining icing.

2. Using a 5-inch spatula, dab a spoonful of base icing in the middle of a cookie and spread it to the edge, pushing the icing away from you instead of dragging and pulling it toward you.

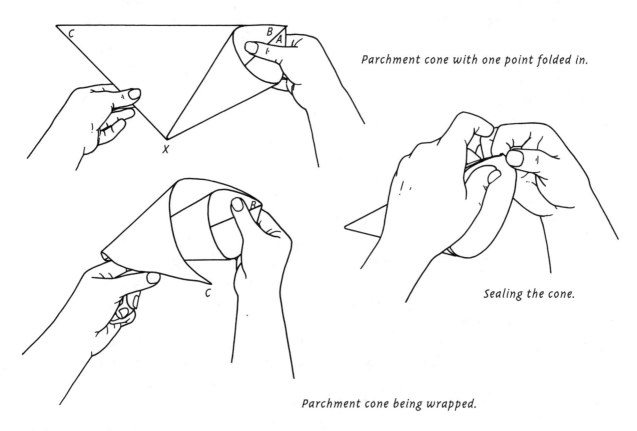

Parchment cone with one point folded in.

Sealing the cone.

Parchment cone being wrapped.

Cover the entire surface, making clean, neat edges. Repeat with all cookies.

If the cookies have several small background areas (for example the soccer ball in photo 3), it may be easier to pipe on the background icing with a #2 or #3 round tip instead of spreading it with a spatula. In fact if you are more comfortable with a decorating bag than with a spatula, you can ice larger areas this way. If you have many cookies to ice, use a large cloth decorating bag; if you are working with a few small areas of background color, try a homemade parchment cone.

If you want to leave spaces on the cookie for a different fill color (like the black spots on a white cow), apply the background color (white) and leave the spots empty. Don't worry if the icing is not completely even; as it dries, it will smooth out, forming a flat surface with slightly rounded edges.

3. Dry the cookies on a rack. Drying time depends on the amount of icing, the humidity of the kitchen, and the outdoor temperature.

When the icing loses its wet look, lightly touch a cookie; if your finger leaves no impression, the cookies are ready for you to add lines, writing, or special piping. Cookies with a lot of base icing may take up to 4 hours to dry. Bare cookies with only a little piping here and there may dry in only 2 hours. Cookies which will have multicolored bases (like the white cow with black spots), should dry for at least 4 hours before the second color is added. The icing must feel smooth and completely firm.

4. Add lines, writing, or other special piping on top of the base coloring.

5. Let the cookies dry again, this time for about 12 hours, though the exact time may vary. Test for dryness by touching the middle of a cookie: The icing is dry when the surface does not break to reveal wet icing underneath.

Method Two: Outlining and Piping

This method involves outlining each cookie, drying it, and then piping in the background with flow icing. It requires a steady hand—I suggest sketching your design on paper before you commit yourself to the actual cookies. Santa's beard and the fur trim of his suit (page 127) use this technique.

1. Choose background and outline colors. Remove enough icing for the outlines and tint the outline colors. Cover and reserve the remaining white icing.

2. Fit a decorating bag with a round #2 tip for small or medium cookies, or a #3 tip for larger ones; fill with the outline icing. Hold the bag in your writing hand at a 45-degree angle, touch the tip to the edge of the cookie and gently squeeze the bag. Raise the tip a bit and, with one steady motion, outline the perimeter of the cookie. To finish a line, stop squeezing the bag, touch the tip to the surface of the outline, and pull the tip up. Finish piping all major lines and let dry, usually about 30 minutes. If you are adding lines or decorations of contrasting colors adjacent to the outlines, you need only let the outlines dry until crusted, but if you are filling adjacent areas with contrasting flow icing, you should let the outlines dry at least two hours.

3. While the outlines are drying, tint the remaining white icing to the base color. Thin this icing with a little water to the consistency of flow icing (see page 28).

4. Fit an icing bag with a #3 tip and fill with the flow icing. Starting on one side of the cookie, pipe the icing inside the outlines, moving the bag back and forth, left and right. The lines of icing should blend together, forming a smooth, slightly convex surface. Stop when the empty space is just covered, or the icing may run over the top of the outline.

5. Dry the cookies on a rack, about 8 hours, though the exact time may vary. The icing is dry when the surface does not break to reveal wet icing underneath.

6. Additional piping and detail can be added on top of the base icing if desired and will require additional drying time.

Method Three: Wet-on-Wet Application

Cookies decorated using this method have dots of flow icing added to a still-wet base coat. The dots can then be modified to form pull-through hearts, shamrocks, stars, or paisley prints.

1. Choose background and decorative colors. Remove enough icing for the decorative details and tint these colors first. Then mix the base color with the remaining icing.

2. Apply a base coat according to Method I, either with a spatula or by piping it on with an icing bag.

3. While the base coat is still wet, pipe on dots; see pages 40–42 for pull-through designs.

Special Piping Techniques

Straight and Curved Lines

TIP SIZE: #2 round for small and medium cookies; #3 for large cookies
BAG POSITION: 45-degree angle, tip on the surface
ICING CONSISTENCY: Outline

To begin, touch the tip to the cookie and gently squeeze the bag. Raise the tip a little and continue squeezing gently while directing the tip where you want the line. To finish, stop squeezing, touch the tip to the surface, and pull up. If the icing is slightly dry, you may get a little peak when you pull up; smooth it down with a small brush dipped in water or a wet fingertip.

Plaid

TIP SIZE: #3 round for verticals; #2 or #1.5 for horizontals. Or use tips that leave flat ribbons of icing
BAG POSITION: 45-degree angle
ICING CONSISTENCY: Outline

Try this technique on a shortbread Scottie dog (page 59) with a well-dried base coat. Lay down equally spaced vertical (flat or round) lines of medium width; let them dry until crusted over. In a contrasting color pipe on thinner horizontal lines. Continue adding verticals and horizontals, letting each set of lines dry before adding another, until the plaid is as detailed as you like. Neaten the edges by piping an outline around the cookie.

Raised Dots and Flat (Polka) Dots

TIP SIZE: #1, #2, or #3 round
BAG POSITION: 90-degree angle, upright; tip just above the surface
ICING CONSISTENCY: Base for raised dots, flow consistency for flat dots

Dots dropped onto a thoroughly dry surface will be raised and slightly rounded. Dots dropped

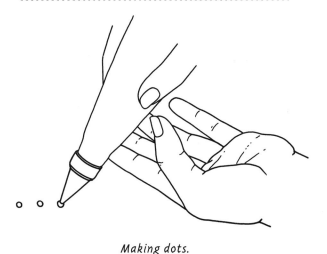

Making dots.

onto a wet surface of flow icing will blend into the surface as flat polka dots.

Place the tip on the cookie and squeeze the bag until you have created a dot of the desired size on the cookie. Release pressure and pull tip away. If any tails pop up on the dots, smooth them down with a wet finger. Recheck the icing consistency and add dribbles of water.

Hearts

TIP SIZE: #1 or #2 round
BAG POSITION: 45-degree angle, slightly above the surface
ICING CONSISTENCY: Base

These are solid heart shapes, not outlines. Squeeze a dot onto the surface. Relax the pressure on the bag and drag the tip down through the dot,

Flower bud with leaf.

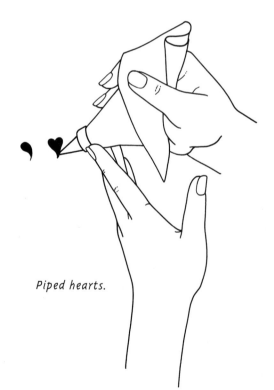

Piped hearts.

Flower bud garland.

pulling it into a teardrop shape, half a heart. Repeat for the other side of the heart.

Flower Buds with Leaves

TIP SIZE: #2 round for leaves, #1 for dot
BAG POSITION: 45-degree angle, sightly above surface
ICING CONSISTENCY: Outline

Squeeze a dot onto the surface. Relax pressure and elongate the bottom of the dot forming a teardrop or bud shape. Carefully pipe a V-shaped leaf at the bottom of the bud. Using a #1 tip, finish the top of the bud with a dot in an accent color.

Flower Bud Garland

TIP SIZE: #2 or #3 round for buds; #1 round for stem
BAG POSITION: 45-degree angle, slightly above surface
ICING CONSISTENCY: Outline

Using a #1 round tip, pipe the main stem for the garland. With a #2 round tip, pipe the buds onto alternate sides of the stem, leaving a slight space between the base of the bud and the stem. With a #1 round tip, add a dot of accent color to the tip of each bud. Let dry 20 minutes. Using a #2 round tip, pipe the V-shaped leaves onto the bottom of each bud, connecting the base of the bud to the garland stem.

Cake Garland

TIP SIZE: #2 round
BAG POSITION: 45-degree angle, sightly above surface
ICING CONSISTENCY: Outline

Pipe a garland of connected U shapes across the entire cookie. Let dry for 10 minutes. Pipe another garland of U shapes overlapping the first but slightly offset. Let dry 10 minutes. Pipe an elongated teardrop into each indentation, starting below the garland and working upward. The fat part of the teardrop is pushed out of the tip first.

Cake garland.

String-of-Pearls Garland

TIP SIZE: #2 round
BAG POSITION: 90-degree angle, vertical; tip just
above surface
ICING CONSISTENCY: Outline

Squeeze a round pearl onto the surface. Relax pressure and pull the icing tip in the direction of the next pearl; squeeze to form the next pearl. If you are right handed, you will probably work left to right. Continue until you have the desired string of pearls.

String-of-pearls garland.

Pull-Through Designs

I first saw this technique on a commercially made cheesecake, where jam hearts were baked right into the batter. I have adapted these pull-through designs to cookies, letting a wet base coat of icing serve as the batter. Choose a toothpick or a skewer to create the lines.

Pull-Through Hearts

TIP SIZE: #2 or #3 round
BAG POSITION: 90-degree angle, vertical; just
above surface
ICING CONSISTENCY: Flow

On a wet base coat, pipe on small dots of a contrasting color. Beginning slightly above the top of the dot, draw the toothpick down and through the center of the dot, pulling out a curved tail that extends into the base coat surrounding the dot. This design may also be made on uniced cookies.

Pull-Through Shamrocks

TIP SIZE: #2 or #3 round
BAG POSITION: 90-degree angle, vertical; just
above surface
ICING CONSISTENCY: Flow

On a wet base coat, using a contrasting color, pipe on 3 dots in the shape of a pyramid. Starting slightly above the top of the dot at the peak of the pyramid, pull the toothpick down through the dot to form a curving tail that extends a little beyond the other 2 dots. Place the tip of the toothpick in the

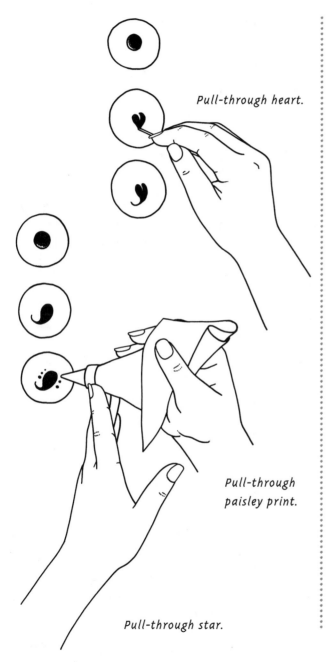

Pull-through heart.

Pull-through paisley print.

Pull-through star.

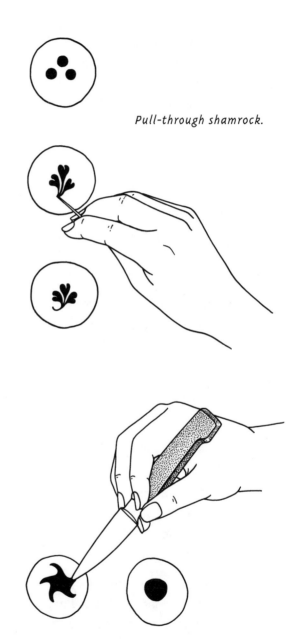

Pull-through shamrock.

Sugarbakers' Cookie Cutter Cookbook

base coat on the left side of the left dot; pull through the dot and downward, joining the tail of the first dot. Repeat with the right dot, beginning on its right, pulling through the dot and downward, joining the tails of the other 2 dots.

Pull-Through Paisley Print

TIP SIZE: #2 or #3 round
BAG POSITION: 90-degree angle, vertical; just above surface
ICING CONSISTENCY: Flow

On a wet base coat, using a contrasting color, pipe on a dot. Insert a toothpick into the middle of the dot and pull out a short, slightly curved tail. Using a #1 tip, pipe on 3 dots on one side of the paisley and then 3 dots on the other side of the paisley.

Pull-Through Star

TIP SIZE: #2 or #3 round
BAG POSITION: 90-degree angle, vertical; just above surface
ICING CONSISTENCY: Flow

On a wet base coat, using a contrasting color, pipe on a dot. Place the pointed end of a paring knife in the middle of the dot; drag out the legs of the star, making them either curved or straight.

Pull-Through Heart Garland

TIP SIZE: #2 or #3 round
BAG POSITION: 90-degree angle, vertical; just above surface
ICING CONSISTENCY: Flow

On a wet base coat, using a contrasting color, pipe on a line of dots. The line can be curved like a garland or straight. Using a toothpick and starting in the base coat slightly outside the first dot, pull down through all the dots, joining them in one continuous line. Do not lift up the toothpick until all the dots are connected and formed into a line of hearts.

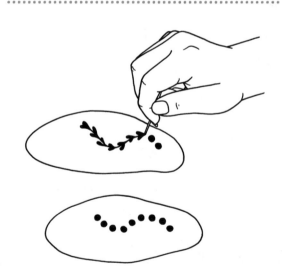

Pull-through heart garland.

Other Decorative Techniques

These techniques don't require a decorating bag; several are simple enough for children.

Sponge-Painting

Spread on a base coat of royal icing and allow it to dry until crusted over (about 30 minutes). Tear a natural sponge in half, exposing a rough surface. Dampen it, then squeeze out the excess water. Dip the rough side into a contrasting colored icing and gently dab it onto the cookie. Use several colors if you wish, letting each color dry thoroughly before sponging on the next.

Shading

Add shading of dry powdered paste color to cookies that have been iced, decorated, and thoroughly dried. Using a dry, clean, artist's paint brush, simply brush on the paste color to achieve the desired shading. I have used this technique to suggest the patina on the Statue of Liberty (page 71).

Decorating with Sugar Dots and Dragées

Apply these purchased decorations to a wet base coat that has not begun to set. Otherwise the decorations will not stick.

Decorating with Tinted Sugars

Choose crystals of different sizes and dye them to meet your own needs.

Dyeing sugar crystals: Estimate the quantity of sugar you will need and set it aside. Dip a toothpick into powdered food color and then stir into the sugar crystals. Begin with a very small amount of dye and add more to intensify the shade. Add more sugar crystals to tone down a color that is too intense.

Sugaring: Add enough water to 2 tablespoons of meringue powder to achieve the consistency of lightly beaten egg white. With a small paintbrush or pastry brush, paint cookies with the mixture where you want the sugar to stick. Sprinkle the sugar over the cookies; let cookies dry for 10 minutes before shaking off the excess. When the surface has dried completely, you can pipe on outlines to add detail and definition to the sugared areas.

Sugar dusting: Sprinkling fine-grained sugar (tinted or white) on top of wet icing produces a surface that looks like flocked velvet. The technique is not recommended for cookies that will be shipped, since the sugar may fall off. Spread or pipe on a base coat of royal icing; sprinkle sugar over the icing while it is still wet. Let the cookies dry for 45 minutes before shaking off excess sugar.

A Cookie Calendar:

Twelve Months of Cookie Cutter Cookies

January

February

March

April

May

June

July

August

September

October

November

December

Almond Nut-Crunch Cookies

I live in southern Oregon, the state that produces almost all of the nation's hazelnuts; not far south is California's almond-growing region. In the midst of this bounty you can understand that at Christmas our nut bowl overflows. In January, I use the leftovers to make these crunchy cookies.

Almonds are best freshly picked or only a few months old. The flavor of ground unsalted, unskinned almonds, familiar from Amaretto liqueur, blends well with butter and vanilla and is sublime in baked goods. If you substitute skinned hazelnuts for the almonds, these cookies will be a little browner.

1 cup (2 sticks) unsalted butter, at room temperature	**2 cups flour**
3/4 cup sugar	**1 1/4 cups finely ground, blanched or natural unsalted almonds (about 2 cups whole almond pieces)**
1 teaspoon vanilla extract	
2 large egg yolks	

1. In a large bowl, using a mixer, beat the butter and sugar until creamy, about 3 minutes. Beat in the vanilla extract and egg yolks until thoroughly combined. Add the flour and nuts, and mix well. If the ingredients do not come together to form a dough, knead the mixture with your hands until a dough forms, about 1 minute.

2. Shape the dough into a large disk. Wrap it tightly in plastic wrap or place in a reclosable plastic bag. Refrigerate for at least 1 hour but no more than 2 hours.

continued on next page

Cookie Crumbs— Almond Nut-Crunch Cookie Variation

For Valentine's Day, Mother's Day, Sweet Sixteen, or any holiday where love is a theme, I cut these cookies into hearts and sandwich them around a layer of jam.

Use 2 heart cutters: a large cutter (at least 3 inches) and a smaller one (1 to 1 1/2 inches). Cut all the dough into 3-inch hearts and place on parchment sheets. Cut a small heart from the center of half the large hearts. Remove the small heart cutouts to a separate parchment sheet.

Bake all cookies as directed. When completely cool, frost the solid large hearts with raspberry jam. Sift confectioners' sugar over the small hearts and the cookies with heart-shaped holes. Gently sandwich to-

continued on next page

*gether the large jam-covered
hearts and the cookies with
heart-shaped holes. Pipe
dots of pink royal icing on
the small hearts or serve
them plain. These cookies get
soggy quickly, so eat them
the day they are made.*

Suggested Cutters

*Any New Year's motif:
Father Time, Baby New
Year, top hat, clock
striking midnight. Also:
heart, snowman, skates.*

Suggested Dough

Any dough

Almond Nut-Crunch Cookies (*cont.*)

3. Preheat the oven to 325° F. Line 2 large baking sheets with parchment.

4. Flour the work surface and rolling pin. Remove half the dough from the plastic; rewrap and refrigerate the remaining half. Roll the dough evenly to a thickness of ¼ inch; cut into shapes. With a spatula, transfer cookie cutouts to prepared baking sheet, keeping them at least 1 inch apart. Repeat rolling and cutting with remaining dough and scraps.

5. Bake 15–20 minutes or until lightly browned. Cool cookies on the baking sheet for 5 minutes, then remove to a rack to cool completely.

 Makes approximately 3 dozen 4-inch cookies. This recipe can easily be doubled.

Snowmen and Minisnowmen

SEE THESE COOKIES IN PHOTO 1 AND ON THE BACK COVER.

WORKING METHOD: Mix master recipe of icing to outline consistency. Divide icing into 8 bowls. Dilute icing with water-meringue powder mixture to desired consistency (see pages 27–28 for consistencies). Tint with paste dye. Keep icing covered when you are not actually using it.

1. For the top hat:
   ICING CONSISTENCY: Base
   ICING COLOR: Black

   Using a spatula (Method I, pages 34–35), spread icing in the hat area. Let dry completely.

2. *For the body and head:*

ICING CONSISTENCY: Base
ICING COLOR: White

Dab icing on the body and head; using a spatula, spread to the edges of the cookie. Let dry completely.

3. *For the scarf:*

ICING CONSISTENCY: Base
ICING COLOR: Red

Using either a spatula or a #2 tip (whichever is easier), spread or pipe on the scarf. Let dry completely.

4. *For the plaid and mittens:*

ICING CONSISTENCY: Outline
ICING COLOR: Lavender

Using a #2 tip, pipe lines of plaid on the scarf. Pipe on the mittens. Let dry to the touch.

5. *For the eyes, mouth, and buttons:*

ICING CONSISTENCY: Outline
ICING COLOR: Black

Using a #2 tip, pipe on the eyes, mouth, and buttons. Let dry to the touch.

6. *For the nose:*

ICING CONSISTENCY: Outline
ICING COLOR: Orange

Using a #1 or #2 tip, pipe on the carrot nose.

continued on next page

Snowmen and Minisnowmen (*cont.*)

7. **For the holly berries:**

ICING CONSISTENCY: Outline
ICING COLOR: Red

Using a #1 tip, pipe holly berries on the hat.

8. **For the holly leaves:**

ICING CONSISTENCY: Outline
ICING COLOR: Green

Using a #1 tip, pipe on holly leaves. Let dry completely.

To make Minisnowmen, follow the same procedure, omitting step 4.

Chowhound Treats for Dogs

After December's excesses, January may not find you in the mood to bake cookies for your family. Fido, however, after weeks of gobbling treats meant for humans, might need some dog-healthy snacks. You can even decorate these treats with royal icing, since small quantities of sugar won't harm dogs. Fido will love these simple cookies and won't care a bit if your decorating is sloppy.

To make a gift for a new dog owner, tuck several cookies into a cellophane bag filled with regular dog food; tie with cord or rustic ribbon. Dog cutters are available by mail order from The Little Fox Factory. (See Mail Order Sources, page 147.)

Cookie Crumbs— Fuzzy Dogs

To give cookie dogs a fuzzy texture, cover them with brown royal icing and dip them into wheat germ or wheat bran while the icing is still wet. Schnauzers and English sheep dogs look especially appealing. Then pipe on toe nails and dark brown or black eyes.

Suggested Cutters

All breeds, sizes, and shapes of dogs; bones, shoes, balls, and steaks.

5 cups whole-wheat flour	3/4 cup shortening or nonrancid meat drippings or bacon grease
1 cup powdered milk solids	
2 teaspoons garlic powder	2 large eggs
2 tablespoons wheat germ	1 3/4 cups water
2 teaspoons beef-bouillon granules	

1. Preheat the oven to 350° F. In a large mixing bowl combine the flour, powdered milk solids, garlic powder, wheat germ, and beef-bouillon granules. Stir to blend. With a pastry cutter, cut in the shortening.

2. Make a well in the center of the dry ingredients and add the eggs and water all at once. With a large spoon, stir until a dough forms. If the dough seems dry and cracked, add dribbles of water until the dough is workable.

3. Turn the dough onto a lightly floured surface and knead until smooth, about 2 minutes. With a lightly floured rolling pin, roll the dough to a uniform thickness of 1/3 inch. Cut into shapes. With a spatula, transfer to a lightly greased baking sheet, keeping the cookies at least 1 inch apart. Roll and cut remaining dough and scraps.

4. Bake 30 minutes or until hard and medium brown. Cool on a wire rack.

 Makes approximately 5 dozen 3-inch doggie treats.

Cookie Crumbs— Gift Baskets

Making a gift basket for that special someone should be a labor of love. For a charming presentation, buy high-quality handmade chocolate truffles, candies, or jelly beans, and tuck them into the basket along with your homemade cookies. You can embellish the presentation with wrapping paper, ribbons, or gift bags.

Suggested Cutters

Hearts, lips, cupids, roses, any Halloween or Easter motif.

Chocolate Cherry Valentine Thins

Chocolate is a must for Valentine cookies. Make hearts, cupids, and arrows from this luscious, tender dough and give them as Valentines to a special friend, teacher, or lover. Tuck them in lunch pails, or bake them on wooden dowels and make cookie pops for a bouquet (page 138). For a thoughtful gift, arrange the cookie pops with colored tissue paper in a small narrow vase or cookie jar, add a card, and deliver it in person. You can also use this dough for chocolate bunnies or eggs for Easter. Decorate them, tuck into a cellophane bag, and hide them with the Easter eggs on the lawn.

These cookies can be made a week in advance. If you allow them to cool completely on the cookie sheet, they will become firmer and can stand up to extra handling.

---

1 ¹/₂ cups (3 sticks) unsalted butter, room temperature

2 ¹/₂ cups confectioners' sugar

2 large eggs

1 teaspoon vanilla extract

3 cups bleached all-purpose flour

1 cup Dutch-process cocoa

¹/₄ teaspoon salt

¹/₂ teaspoon ground cinnamon

¹/₂ cup minced sour dried cherries

---

1. In a large bowl, using a mixer, beat the butter and sugar until all of the sugar is absorbed into the butter, about 3 minutes. Add the eggs and vanilla and continue to beat until light and fluffy, about 4 minutes.

2. In a medium bowl, combine the flour, cocoa, salt, and cinnamon. Stir to blend.

3. Add the flour mixture to the butter mixture and beat until the flour is absorbed into the butter and forms a mass. Beat well for 2 minutes to combine thoroughly. Fold in the cherries. Scrape the dough onto a large sheet of plastic wrap or into a reclosable plastic bag. Wrap tightly and refrigerate for at least 2 hours.

4. Preheat the oven to 350° F. Flour the work surface and rolling pin; remove half the dough from the plastic; rewrap and refrigerate the remaining half. Roll dough to a thickness of 1/4 inch and cut into shapes, making sure to cut cleanly through any bits of cherry. With a spatula, transfer cookie cutouts to an ungreased baking sheet, keeping them at least 1 inch apart. Form scraps into a ball and chill for 15 minutes. Roll and cut remaining dough and scraps.

5. Bake 10–12 minutes for soft cookies; transfer cookies immediately from the baking sheet to a wire rack to cool completely. Bake 13–15 minutes for crisp cookies; allow cookies to cool completely on the baking sheet.

 Makes approximately 4 1/2 dozen 3-inch cookies. This recipe can easily be doubled.

Sweet Cherry Treats

These tender tea cookies, rich in butter and flecked with bursts of color, are true dazzlers; the combination of butter and oil makes them meltingly tender. They look beautiful, either decorated with royal icing or left plain. They are so good that you don't even have to add the cherries to the dough. I know you will want to make them over and over again.

Use this dough for Valentine's Day, President's Day, St. Patrick's Day, Christmas, or July 4th—any holiday where red- or green-flecked cookies are appropriate. Try mixing red and green cherries in Christmas cookies, or marbleize flecked dough with a solid-colored dough.

continued on next page

Flour your work surface and rolling pin heavily to control the stickiness of the cherries.

¹/₂ cup confectioners' sugar	2 ³/₄ cups bleached all-purpose flour
¹/₂ cup granulated sugar	¹/₂ teaspoon cream of tartar
¹/₂ cup vegetable oil	¹/₂ teaspoon baking soda
¹/₂ cup (1 stick) unsalted butter	1 cup maraschino or glacé cherries, chopped by hand or in the food processor (be careful not to overprocess), and blotted dry on paper towels
1 large egg	
¹/₂ teaspoon vanilla extract	
¹/₂ teaspoon almond extract (optional)	

1. With a mixer, cream the sugars, oil, and butter together until almost smooth, about 5 minutes. Add the egg and extract(s). Beat well.

2. In a small mixing bowl, combine the flour, cream of tartar, and baking soda, and stir to blend. Add to the butter mixture and mix well.

3. With a large spatula, fold in the cherries. Wrap the dough in plastic wrap or put it in a reclosable plastic bag. Refrigerate for at least 3 hours or overnight.

4. Preheat the oven to 350° F. Flour the work surface and rolling pin. Remove half the dough from the plastic, rewrapping and refrigerating the unused portion. Roll dough to a thickness of ³/₈ inch and cut into shapes, pressing down hard on the cutter to cut cleanly through any bits of cherry. With a spatula, transfer cookie cutouts to an ungreased baking sheet, keeping them at least 2 inches apart. Form scraps into a ball and chill. Roll and cut remaining dough and scraps.

5. Bake 10 minutes or until the bottoms are barely browned. Cool cookies on the baking sheet for 5 minutes and then transfer to a rack.

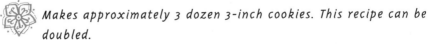 *Makes approximately 3 dozen 3-inch cookies. This recipe can be doubled.*

Coconut Nobbies

*T*oasted coconut tastes so marvelous that I couldn't resist adding it to a dough for cookie cutters. At Easter I use it for sheep cookies because the nubby surfaces resemble fleece. This easy dough, suitable for beginners, also makes charming cookie dogs and farm animals, which need very little decoration.

1 cup lightly toasted, flaked coconut, cooled to room temperature	3/4 cup (1 1/2 sticks) cold unsalted butter, cut into tablespoon-size chunks
1 cup sugar	2 large eggs
2 1/4 cups bleached all-purpose flour	1/2 teaspoon vanilla extract
	2 tablespoons milk (optional)

1. In a food processor fitted with a steel blade, combine the coconut and sugar. Process until the coconut is coarsely ground. Pour the coconut-sugar mixture into a medium mixing bowl. Wipe out the processor bowl with a paper towel and return it and the blade to the processor base.

2. Combine the flour and butter in the processor; process until the mixture is well blended and reduced to fine crumbs, about 30 seconds.

3. Add the flour-butter mixture to the coconut-sugar mixture. With a large wooden spoon, stir to combine. Add the eggs and vanilla extract. Knead the mixture with your hands until a dough forms. If the mixture seems dry and does not mass easily into a dough, sprinkle the milk over the ingredients until a pliable dough forms.

continued on next page

Cookie Crumbs— Cookies for Ornaments, Shipping, and Everyday Eating

Almost any dough can be made into an ornament or can survive the hard knocks of shipping if you treat the cookies properly:

1. Allow the cookies to cool completely on the baking sheets. The heat will dry out the interiors and crisp the exteriors.

2. Before decorating with royal icing, allow the cookies to sit uncovered overnight. Or place the cookies in the cooled oven and leave them there overnight.

Suggested Cutters

Sheep, dogs, cows, chickens, clowns, teddy bears, or anything that should look cuddly.

Coconut Nobbies (*cont.*)

4. Turn the dough onto a large piece of plastic wrap or place it in a reclosable plastic bag. Refrigerate for 30 minutes. Meanwhile, preheat the oven to 375° F. Lightly grease 2 large baking sheets or line them with parchment paper.

5. Generously flour the work surface and rolling pin. Remove half the chilled dough from the plastic; rewrap and refrigerate the remaining half. Roll the dough to a thickness of $1/4$ inch and cut into shapes. With a spatula, transfer cookie cutouts to the prepared baking sheets keeping cookies at least 1 inch apart. Form scraps into a ball and chill. Roll and cut remaining dough and scraps.

6. Bake, 1 sheet at a time, 8–10 minutes, until the centers of the cookies are firm and the bottoms are very lightly browned. Cool on the baking sheet for 5 minutes and then transfer to racks to cool completely.

 Makes approximately 2 dozen 3-inch cookies.

*M*iniature *B*aby *B*ears

SEE THESE COOKIES IN PHOTO 7.

WORKING METHOD: Mix master recipe of icing to outline consistency. Divide icing into 3 bowls. Dilute with water-meringue powder mixture to desired consistencies (see pages 27–28 for consistencies). Tint with paste dye. Keep icing covered when you are not actually using it.

1. *For the diaper:*
ICING CONSISTENCY: Base
ICING COLOR: White

Using a spatula or a #2 tip, whichever is easier, spread or pipe on a diaper.

2. For the bow tie or hair bow:

ICING CONSISTENCY: Outline

ICING COLOR: Pink for girl bears or light blue for boys

Using a #1 tip, pipe on a bow tie for the boys or a hair bow for the girls.

3. For the belly button:

ICING CONSISTENCY: Outline

ICING COLOR: Beige or flesh color

Using a #1 tip, pipe on a belly button. Let dry completely.

Mrs. Harlan's Highbrow Shortbread

In 1956, Mrs. Harlan was the most entertaining hostess in Richmond, Kentucky, whose gracious parties were in a class by themselves. These mouth-watering shortbreads appeared on her table at dinner parties, luncheons, and teas. Later she passed down the recipe to my grandmother, who owned the Blue Rib Inn in Louisville. She served Mrs. Harlan's shortbreads after dinner as a palate-cooling complement to her great barbecue. Now, in the tradition of Southern hospitality, I share the recipe with you.

Decorate these cookies any way you please. Made of only 3 ingredients, they bake without changing their shape at all whether they have been cut thick (½ inch) or thin (¼ inch).

---

1 cup (2 sticks) unsalted butter	2 ½ cups bleached all-purpose flour
5/8 cup sugar (½ cup plus 2 tablespoons)	

---

continued on next page

1. In a large mixing bowl, using an electric mixer, beat the butter and sugar until creamy. Stir in the flour by hand, mixing thoroughly.

2. Turn the dough onto a large piece of plastic wrap or place it in a reclosable plastic bag. Refrigerate for 1 hour. Meanwhile, preheat the oven to 300° F.

3. Lightly flour the work surface and rolling pin. Remove half the chilled dough from the plastic; rewrap and refrigerate the remaining half. Roll the dough to a thickness of $^1/_4$–$^1/_2$ inch and cut into shapes. With a spatula, transfer shortbread cutouts to an un-greased baking sheet, keeping them at least 1 inch apart. Form scraps into a ball and chill. Roll and cut remaining dough and scraps.

4. Bake 20–25 minutes or until the cookies spring back when touched lightly; they should not brown. Cool on the baking sheet for 3 minutes and then carefully transfer to a rack to cool completely.

 Makes about 2 dozen 3-inch cookies.

Pansies

SEE THESE COOKIES IN PHOTO 2.

WORKING METHOD: Mix master recipe of icing to outline consistency. Divide icing into 4 bowls. Dilute with water-meringue powder mixture to the required consistency (see pages 27–28 for consistencies). Tint with paste dye. Keep icing covered when you are not actually using it.

Suggested Cutters

Any motif that suggests pastel colors or would be attractive with a white base; any shape with finely detailed edges; any spring or summer motif.

Suggested Dough

Sugar cookie or short-bread

1. For the background:
ICING CONSISTENCY: Base
ICING COLOR: Delicate pastel yellow or lavender.

Apply base with a spatula (Method I, pages 34–35).

2. For the petal outlines:
ICING CONSISTENCY: Flow
ICING COLOR: Yellow or lavender, 2 or 3 shades darker than base, or in contrasting color

Tint icing for petal outlines while the base icing is still wet. Using a #1 or #2 tip, pipe an outline of the darker icing around the outside of the cookie. Make the individual petals by piping lines in to the center of the flower. Let dry to the touch.

3. For the accents:
ICING CONSISTENCY: Outline
ICING COLOR: Dark brown, black, or another dark accent color

With a #1 or #2 tip, pipe accents around some of the petal forms. Add pansy markings, the short curved lines that radiate outward from the center of the flower. Let dry to the touch.

4. For the flower centers:
ICING CONSISTENCY: Outline
ICING COLOR: Same as base coat

Using a #1 tip, pipe a small circle in the middle of the pansy. Let dry completely. If you wish to fill in the center with the accent color, pipe in remaining icing from step 3 using a #1 tip.

To further highlight the pansy center, brush on contrasting powdered dry food coloring after the icing is completely dry.

Bluebirds

SEE THESE COOKIES IN PHOTO **2**.

WORKING METHOD: Mix master recipe of icing to outline consistency. Divide icing into 5 bowls. Dilute with water-meringue powder mixture to desired consistency (see pages 27–28 for consistencies). Tint with paste dye. Keep icing covered when you are not actually using it.

1. *For the background:*
ICING CONSISTENCY: Base
ICING COLOR: Light blue

Apply base coat using a spatula (Method I, pages 34–35), leaving beak and feet bare.

2. *For the beak:*
ICING CONSISTENCY: Base
ICING COLOR: Yellow

Using a #1 tip, pipe on the beak. Let dry to the touch.

Bluebird.

Suggested Dough

Sugar cookie or short-bread

3. *For the feet:*
ICING CONSISTENCY: Outline
ICING COLOR: Brown

Using a #1 tip, pipe on claws in the shape of an inverted pitchfork.

4. *For the tuft, wing markings, and tail feathers:*
ICING CONSISTENCY: Outline
ICING COLOR: Blue, several shades darker than base coat

Using a #1 or #2 tip, pipe on tail feathers, wing markings, and a tuft at the top of the head.

5. *For the eye:*
ICING CONSISTENCY: Outline
ICING COLORS: Black

Using a #1 tip, pipe on the eye. Let dry completely.

Scottie Dogs

SEE THIS COOKIE IN PHOTO 5.

WORKING METHOD: Mix master recipe of icing to outline consistency. Divide icing into 4 bowls. Dilute icing with water-meringue powder mixture to desired consistency (see pages 27–28 for consistencies). Tint with paste dye. Keep icing covered when you are not actually using it.

1. *For the colored vertical lines:*
ICING CONSISTENCY: Outline
ICING COLORS: Pink, peach, dark green, and white

continued on next page

Suggested Dough

Shortbread or sugar-cookie dough

Scottie Dogs (*cont.*)

Using a #2 tip, pipe vertical lines from the top of the dog to the bottom, alternating the 3 colors. Reserve icing for the horizontal lines.

2. For the white verticals:
Using a small nonserrated ribbon tip, pipe on the white vertical lines. Let dry to the touch.

3. For the horizontals:
Using the reserved icing and the same tips, pipe horizontal lines from one side of the cookie to the other, alternating the 4 colors.

4. For the eye:
Make the eye by pressing a gold or silver dragée into the icing while icing is still wet. Let dry completely.

Old-Fashioned Vanilla Sugar Cookies

*T*uck these delicate cookies into an Easter basket, or give them away as favors at weddings, baby showers, or spring parties. They look sweet and innocent decorated with pastel royal icing and cut into such shapes as bunnies, eggs, and teddy bears. Make extra, they disappear fast!

³/₄ cup sugar	1 teaspoon vanilla extract
6 tablespoons unsalted butter	2 cups bleached all-purpose flour
¹/₃ cup shortening	1 ¹/₂ teaspoons baking powder
1 large egg	¹/₄ teaspoon salt
1 tablespoon milk	

1. With a mixer, cream the sugar, butter, and shortening until fluffy. Add the egg, milk, and vanilla, and beat well.

2. In a small mixing bowl, combine the flour, baking powder, and salt, and stir to blend. Add to the butter mixture and mix on medium speed until thoroughly combined.

3. Turn the dough onto a large piece of plastic wrap or place in a reclosable plastic bag. Refrigerate for at least 2 hours or overnight.

4. Preheat the oven to 375° F. Flour the work surface and rolling pin. Remove half the chilled dough from the plastic; rewrap and refrigerate the remaining half. If the

continued on next page

Cookie Crumbs— Real Grass Easter Baskets

Nestle Easter goodies in baskets lined with real grass, not artificial. Spray paint a natural basket using a pastel spring color, or leave it plain. Line the basket with a heavy-duty clear plastic bag and add 1 inch of dirt. About 3 weeks before Easter, sow rye-grass seed on the dirt. Set the basket in front of a sunny window, and water it lightly every other day until the seeds sprout. In 2 to 3 weeks you will have a thick carpet of spring grass. Stop watering the basket 2 days before Easter. Place the cookies in clear cellophane bags and tie the tops with pretty ribbons. Fill the spaces between the cookies with handmade truffles, chocolate, bunnies, jelly beans, and eggs.

dough was refrigerated overnight, let it sit on the counter for about 30 minutes, or until it becomes pliable and easy to handle.

5. Roll the dough to a thickness of ¼ inch and cut into shapes. With a spatula, transfer cookie cutouts to an ungreased baking sheet, keeping them at least inches apart. Form the scraps into a ball and chill. Roll and cut remaining dough and scraps.

6. Bake 8–10 minutes or just until edges start to brown lightly. Cool on the baking sheet for 3 minutes and transfer with a spatula to racks to cool completely.

 Makes approximately 3 dozen 3-inch cookies or 16 oversized cookies. This recipe can easily be doubled.

Pink **D**otted **S**wiss **H**earts

SEE THIS COOKIE IN PHOTO 7.

WORKING METHOD: Mix master recipe of icing to outline consistency. Divide icing into 3 bowls. Dilute with water-meringue powder mixture to desired consistencies (see pages 27–28). Tint with paste dye. Keep icing covered when you are not actually using it. These cookies are made by outlining and then filling the interior.

1. **For the outer zigzag and dots:**
   ICING CONSISTENCY: Outline
   ICING COLOR: White

   Using a #2 tip, pipe a zigzag line around the outer edge of the cookie. Let dry to the touch. Still using the #2 tip, pipe a dot in the middle of each "ruffle." Let dry to the touch. Reserve white icing for stitching and bow.

Suggested Cutters

Any shape appropriate for Easter, Mother's Day, weddings, or baby showers; any spring or summer, Chanukah, or Christmas motif.

Suggested Dough

Any sugar cookie or shortbread dough

2. For the inner heart outline:

ICING CONSISTENCY: Outline
ICING COLOR: Pale pink

Using a #2 tip, pipe a heart outline inside the zigzag. Reserve icing for the dots.

3. For the base coat:

ICING CONSISTENCY: Base
ICING COLOR: Pale pink

Using a spatula, carefully spread dabs of icing inside the pink heart outline to fill the interior. Let dry to the touch.

4. For the stitching and bow:

Using the reserved white icing (step 1) and a #2 tip, pipe a broken line to look like stitching close to the pink outline. Pipe a bow at the top of the heart.

5. For the interior dots:

Using the reserved pale pink icing (step 2), and a #1 or #2 tip, pipe dots randomly across the pink heart. Let dry completely.

Hearts with Swirls and Ruffles

SEE THIS COOKIE IN PHOTO 7.

WORKING METHOD: Cut the hearts with a zigzag or ruffled cutter. Mix master recipe of icing to outline consistency. Divide icing into 2 bowls. Dilute with water-meringue powder mixture to desired consistencies (see pages 27–28). Tint with paste dye. Keep icing covered when you are not actually using it. You must apply the pull-through hearts before the base coat dries (see page 41).

continued on next page

Suggested Dough

Any shortbread or sugar-cookie dough

Hearts with Swirls and Ruffles (*cont.*)

1. For the zigzag:
ICING CONSISTENCY: Outline
ICING COLOR: White

Using a #2 tip, pipe a zigzag line around the edge of the heart. Reserve icing for the inner zigzag.

2. For the base coat:
ICING CONSISTENCY: Base
ICING COLOR: White

Using a spatula (Method I, pages 34–35), gently spread dabs of icing just to the edge of the zigzag border.

3. For the red hearts:
ICING CONSISTENCY: Flow
ICING COLOR: Red

Working quickly before the base coat has any chance to dry, drop dots of red flow icing randomly on the surface of the wet cookie. With a toothpick, make a garland of pull-through hearts with long tails (see page 42). Let dry completely.

4. For the inner zigzag:
Using the reserved white outline icing (step 1), and a #2 tip, pipe an elongated zigzag line inside the first zigzag on top of the base coat icing. Let dry completely.

Hearts with Flower Buds

SEE THIS COOKIE ON THE BACK COVER.

WORKING METHOD: Mix master recipe of icing to outline consistency. Divide icing into 5 bowls. Dilute with water-meringue powder mixture to desired consistencies (see pages 27–28). Tint with paste dye. Keep icing covered when you are not actually using it.

1. **For the zigzag border:**
ICING CONSISTENCY: Outline
ICING COLOR: White

Using a #1 or #2 tip, pipe an outline around the zigzag edge of the heart. Let dry to the touch.

2. **For the base coat:**
ICING CONSISTENCY: Base
ICING COLOR: White

Using a spatula, dab icing in the middle of the cookie and spread gently to the edge (Method I, pages 34–35); stop just short of the zigzag line. Let dry completely.

3. **For the flower buds:**
ICING CONSISTENCY: Outline
ICING COLOR: Red

Using a #2 tip, pipe on flower buds (see page 38).

4. **For the bud tips:**
ICING CONSISTENCY: Outline
ICING COLOR: Dark red

Using a #1 tip, pipe accents at the tips of the flower buds. Let dry to the touch.

continued on next page

Suggested Dough

Any butter shortbread or sugar cookie dough

Hearts with Flower Buds (*cont.*)

5. For the leaves:

ICING CONSISTENCY: Outline
ICING COLOR: Leaf green

Using a #1 tip, pipe on leaves. Let dry completely.

Zigzag Hearts on Ribbons

SEE THIS COOKIES ON THE FRONT COVER.

WORKING METHOD: Using a power drill with a clean 1/16-inch bit, drill 10–12 holes about 1/2 inch from the cookie edge, following the heart-shaped outline of the cookie. Then mix master recipe of icing to outline consistency. Dilute with water-meringue powder mixture to desired consistencies (see pages 27–28 for consistencies). Keep icing covered when you are not actually using it.

(see pages 27–28 for consistencies)

1. For the dots, zigzags, and small hearts:

ICING CONSISTENCY: Outline
ICING COLOR: White

Using a #1 tip, pipe white dots around each drilled hole. Pipe a zigzag outline around the cookie edge. Let dry to the touch.

Pipe small hearts (page 38) in the middle of the cookie and around the edge between the holes and the zigzag border. The hearts fit best if piped into every other angle. Let dry completely.

Pipe small hearts (page 38)

2. For the ribbon:

Cut a piece of thin pink ribbon about 24 inches long. Starting at the top of the cookie, and leaving an 8-inch tail, thread the ribbon through the holes; there should be another 8-inch end left over. Tie the ribbon ends into a bow at the top of the cookie.

Suggested Dough

Any light-colored shortbread or sugar-cookie dough

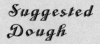

Easter Eggs à la Fabergé

SEE THESE COOKIES IN PHOTO 2.

WORKING METHOD: Mix master recipe of icing to outline consistency. Divide icing into 3 bowls. Dilute icing with water-meringue powder mixture to the required consistencies (see pages 27—28 for icing consistencies). Tint with paste dye. Keep icing covered when you are not actually using it.

*Suggested
Dough*

Sugar cookie, short-bread, or chocolate shortbread

1. For the background:
ICING CONSISTENCY: Base
ICING COLOR: Any delicate pastel

Apply base with a spatula (Method I, pages 34—35).

2. For the diagonals:
ICING CONSISTENCY: Outline
ICING COLOR: White

Using a #2 tip, pipe diagonal lines from one side of the egg to the other. Then form a crosshatch design by piping a second set of diagonals that intersect the first in diamond shapes. Let dry to the touch.

3. For the dots:
ICING CONSISTENCY: Outline
ICING COLORS: Pastel shades of lavender, pink, and yellow

Using a #2 tip, pipe 1 dot in each diamond shape. Let dry completely.

Cookie Crumbs— An Easy Nonstick Surface

To make a nonstick surface for rolling dough, wet your countertop and cover with a sheet of waxed paper (or plastic wrap). Lightly flour the paper. The paper will stick to the wet counter, but the cookie dough won't stick to the floured paper.

Suggested Cutters

Any motif suggesting spring, Easter, Mother's Day, Father's Day, weddings, birthdays, or summer (sun, lobsters, light house, Statue of Liberty).

Lemon Crisps for Spring

 The tart lemon flavor of these crisp cookies will rouse your taste buds after a long winter.

3 ³/₄ cups sifted bleached all-purpose flour	¹/₂ cup unsalted butter
1 ¹/₂ teaspoons baking powder	1 ¹/₂ cups sugar
1 teaspoon salt	2 teaspoons lemon extract
¹/₂ cup shortening	2 large eggs
	Zest of 2 lemons, minced fine

1. In a small mixing bowl, combine the sifted flour, baking powder, and salt. Stir to blend.

2. With a mixer, using a large bowl, beat the shortening, butter, sugar, and lemon extract until creamy. Beat in the eggs and lemon peel.

3. Gradually add the flour mixture to the shortening mixture and beat until thoroughly combined. Continue beating until a dough forms, about 2 minutes. If the dough does not form, turn off the mixer and push and blend the ingredients together with a large spoon until they mass into a dough.

4. Turn the dough onto a large piece of plastic wrap or place it in a reclosable plastic bag. Refrigerate for 30 minutes. Meanwhile, preheat the oven to 375° F.

5. Lightly flour the work surface and rolling pin. Remove half the dough from the plastic; rewrap and refrigerate the other half. Roll to a thickness of 1/4 inch and cut into shapes, pressing down hard on the cutter to cut cleanly through any bits of lemon

peel. With a spatula, transfer cookie cutouts to an ungreased baking sheet, keeping them at least 1 inch apart. Form scraps into a ball and chill. Roll and cut remaining dough and scraps.

6. Bake 10–12 minutes or until golden brown. Cool the cookies on the baking sheet for 3 minutes and then carefully transfer to a rack to cool completely.

 Makes approximately 5 dozen 3-inch cookies.

*L*obsters

SEE THIS COOKIE IN PHOTO 8.

WORKING METHOD: Mix master recipe of icing to outline consistency. Divide icing into 3 bowls. Dilute with water-meringue powder mixture to desired consistencies (see pages 27–28). Tint with paste dye. Keep icing covered when you are not actually using it.

1. *For the base coat:*
ICING CONSISTENCY: Base
ICING COLOR: Deep red

Dab icing in the middle of the cookie and spread gently to the edges (Method I, pages 34–35). Let dry to the touch.

2. *For the outlines:*
ICING CONSISTENCY: Outline
ICING COLOR: Deep red, matching or a shade darker than the base coat

Using a #2 or #3 tip, outline the lobster and pipe lines across the tail. Let dry to the touch.

continued on next page

Suggested Dough

Gingerbread or thick shortbread

Lobsters (*cont.*)

3. **For the eyes:**
   ICING CONSISTENCY: Outline
   ICING COLOR: Black

   Using a #2 tip, pipe on eyes. Let dry completely.

Statue of Liberty Cookies

SEE THIS COOKIE IN PHOTO 8.

WORKING METHOD: Mix master recipe of icing to outline consistency. Divide icing into 4 bowls. Dilute icing with water-meringue powder mixture to desired consistencies (see pages 27–28). Tint with paste dye. Keep icing covered when you are not actually using it.

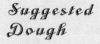

Suggested Dough

Any sturdy dough, such as gingerbread or thick shortbread

1. **For the base coat:**
   ICING CONSISTENCY: Base
   ICING COLOR: Pale green

   Dab icing in the middle of the cookie and spread gently to the edges (Method I, pages 34–35). Do not ice the area where the flames of the torch will be. Let dry to the touch.

2. **For the flames:**
   ICING CONSISTENCY: Base
   ICING COLOR: Medium yellow

   Put a spot of icing on the tip of the torch and spread gently to the edges of the cookie. Let dry to the touch.

3. For the outline, face, and garment folds:

ICING CONSISTENCY: Outline
ICING COLOR: Green, 3 or 4 shades darker than the base coat

Using a #2 tip, outline the statue and pipe on the facial features. Pipe on thicker lines to show the folds in the garment. Let dry to the touch.

4. To outline the flames:

ICING CONSISTENCY: Outline
ICING COLOR: Gold or deep yellow

Using a #2 tip, outline the flames. Place a gold dragée in the middle of the torch, sticking it on with a dot of the gold icing.

5. Optional shading:

To achieve a nice patina, let the cookie dry completely and then gently brush light green powdered dye over the entire surface.

May

Cookie Crumbs— Working with Dowels and Skewers

To make sure that a dowel or skewer will stay put after the cookies have cooled, dab royal icing into the hole. The icing will dry and act as caulking.

Suggested Cutters

Any motifs that suggest Mother's Day or Father's Day, May Day, spring. Any cookie that will look attractive on a stick as part of a bouquet.

Cream-Cheese Sugar Cookies for May Day and Mother's Day

*B*oth *Mothers* and *Fathers* appreciate receiving these cookies on their special day. Choose hearts, pansies, and other flowers for Mother. For Dad try a dozen neckties, each with a slightly different design.

This dough also works well for making cookies-on-a-stick using wooden skewers or dowels, available at most craft stores. Substitute the cookie pops for flowers in cookie bouquets or use them in decorative theme baskets, for example for an "over-the-hill" birthday party or a baby shower. Add balloons, tissue paper, and colored ribbons, and the basket makes a sprightly centerpiece for the table.

---

3 ¹/₂ cups bleached all-purpose flour

1 teaspoon baking powder

1 8-ounce package cream cheese, room temperature

1 cup (2 sticks) unsalted butter

2 cups sugar

1 large egg

1 teaspoon vanilla

¹/₂ teaspoon almond extract

Wooden sticks or dowels about 12 inches long (optional)

---

1. In a small mixing bowl, combine the flour and baking powder, and stir to blend.

2. In a large mixing bowl, beat the cream cheese, butter, and sugar until creamy and light, about 2 minutes. Add the egg, vanilla extract, and almond extract and mix for 30 seconds.

3. Add the flour mixture to the butter mixture and mix until ingredients are combined but still lumpy. Turn the dough onto a large piece of plastic wrap or place it in a re-closable plastic bag. Knead the dough inside the plastic several times, until it is smooth; form it into a disk 2 inches thick. Refrigerate for at least 2 hours or overnight.

4. Preheat the oven to 375° F. Lightly flour the work surface and rolling pin. Remove half the dough from the plastic; rewrap and refrigerate the remaining half. Roll the dough to a thickness of $1/4$ inch and cut into shapes. With a spatula, transfer cookie cutouts to an ungreased baking sheet, keeping them at least 1 inch apart. Form scraps into a ball and chill. Roll and cut remaining dough and scraps.

5. To make cookies-on-a-stick, carefully insert a dowel or skewer into the center of each cookie. (If you are using skewers, put the blunt end into the cookie.) Press the dough gently around the entry point so that the cookie will bake tightly around the stick.

6. Bake 8–10 minutes or until the edges are firm and lightly browned. Cool the cookies on the baking sheet for 5 minutes and then transfer them with a spatula to a rack to cool completely.

 Makes approximately 4 dozen 3-inch cookies.

Rocking Horses

SEE THIS COOKIE ON THE BACK COVER.

WORKING METHOD: Mix master recipe of icing to outline consistency. Divide icing into 5 bowls. Dilute with water-meringue powder mixture to desired consistencies (see pages 27–28). Tint with paste dye. Keep icing covered when you are not actually using it.

continued on next page

Suggested Dough

Sugar cookie or short-bread

Rocking Horses (*cont.*)

1. *To outline the rocker:*
ICING CONSISTENCY: Outline
ICING COLOR: White

Using a #2 tip, outline the rocker. Reserve some icing for the mane and rocker decorations. Let dry completely.

2. *To fill in the rocker:*
ICING CONSISTENCY: Flow
ICING COLOR: Light blue

Using a #2 tip, fill in the rocker outline, moving the decorating bag back and forth as you work (Method II, pages 35–36). Let dry to the touch.

3. *For the top edge of the rocker and the tail:*
ICING CONSISTENCY: Outline
ICING COLOR: Light pink

Using a #2 tip, pipe a line against the top edge of the rocker. Pipe on the tail, reserving some icing for the rosebuds. Let icing dry to the touch.

4. *For the mane and rocker decorations:*
Using a #2 tip and the reserved white icing (step 1), pipe on the horse's mane. Pipe on the rocker decorations, dots with short spikes pointing upward. Let dry to the touch.

5. *For the garland stem:*
ICING CONSISTENCY: Outline
ICING COLOR: Pastel green

Using a #2 tip, pipe the garland stem (see page 38) from the nose to the middle of the horse's back, reserving some icing for the leaves. Let dry to the touch.

6. *For the flower buds:*

Using the reserved pink icing and a #2 tip, pipe rosebuds on alternate sides of the garland stem. Let dry to the touch.

7. *For the flower bud tips:*

ICING CONSISTENCY: Outline
ICING COLOR: Medium pink

Using a #1 tip, pipe on the tips of the buds.

8. *For the leaves:*

With the reserved green icing, using a #1 tip, pipe on bud leaves.

P eter R abbit C ookies

SEE THIS COOKIE IN PHOTO 5.

WORKING METHOD: Mix master recipe of icing to outline consistency. Divide icing into 6 bowls. Dilute icing with water-meringue powder mixture to desired consistencies (see pages 27–28). Tint with paste dye. Keep icing covered when you are not actually using it.

1. *For the base coat:*

ICING CONSISTENCY: Base
ICING COLOR: White

With a spatula dab icing on the head and ears, front and back feet, and tail area (Method I, pages 34–35). Gently smooth to the edges. Let dry completely.

continued on next page

Suggested Dough

Shortbread or sugar cookie dough

Peter Rabbit Cookies (*cont.*)

2. *For the jacket:*
ICING CONSISTENCY: Base
ICING COLOR: Light blue

Dab icing in the middle of the cookie and spread to cover the jacket area. Let dry completely.

3. *For the jacket details:*
ICING CONSISTENCY: Outline
ICING COLOR: Sage green

Using a #2 tip, pipe on the outlines of the jacket and sleeve. Pipe on the pocket, collar, and buttons. Let dry completely.

4. *For the face and ears:*
ICING CONSISTENCY: Outline
ICING COLOR: Pale blush

Using a #2 tip, pipe on the eye, nose, and the line defining the 2 ears. Let dry to the touch.

5. *For the tail and nails:*
ICING CONSISTENCY: Outline
ICING COLOR: White

Using a #2 tip, delineate the cotton tail and the toenails on front and back feet. Pipe 3 dots on the cheek. Let dry to the touch.

6. *For the watch chain:*
ICING CONSISTENCY: Outline
ICING COLOR: Gold

Using a #1 tip, pipe on the watch chain from pocket to sleeve line. Let dry completely.

Lemon Pound-Cake Cutouts

Closely textured pound cake can be cut into cookie shapes or used for petit fours. Make the cake several days ahead and let it set, so that the cookies will be properly firm and dense. I have adapted this recipe from "Harriet and David's Pound Cake," in my book, Dessert in Half the Time.

---

2 3/4 cups flour

1/4 teaspoon soda

1 cup (2 sticks) unsalted butter, room temperature

3 cups sugar

6 large eggs

1 cup sour cream

1/2 teaspoon lemon extract

1 tablespoon lemon juice

2 tablespoons fresh lemon peel, grated and minced

---

1. Preheat the oven to 325° F. Grease and flour two 9-inch loaf pans or one 10-inch tube pan.

2. In a small mixing bowl, combine the flour and soda. Stir to blend.

3. In a large mixing bowl, beat the butter and sugar until light, about 5 minutes. Add the eggs, beating well after each addition.

4. In a glass 2-cup measure stir together the sour cream, lemon extract, lemon juice, and lemon peel.

5. Add the flour mixture and the sour-cream mixture alternately to the butter mixture, beginning and ending with the flour mixture. Beat at low speed after each addition until just combined. Do not overmix.

continued on next page

Cookie Crumbs— A Simple Chocolate Glaze

Semisweet chocolate melted with a little shortening makes a delectable substitute for icing. Try about 1/2 teaspoon of shortening with 8 ounces of chocolate. Melt the chocolate-shortening mixture over hot, not simmering, water in a double boiler. Glaze the cookies with the chocolate, or use it in a parchment icing cone for writing script.

Suggested Cookie Cutters

Any motif suitable for pastel colors, including designs relating to Mother's Day, Easter, spring, weddings, and baby showers.

Lemon Pound-Cake Cutouts (*cont.*)

6. Pour the batter into the prepared pan(s). Bake on the middle rack of the preheated oven until a tester inserted near the center comes out clean, 75–90 minutes for metal pans, 65–80 minutes for glass pans. Cool on a wire rack for 15 minutes. Remove cake from pans and cool completely, preferably for 24 hours, before slicing and cutting.

To Cut the Cookies:

1. With a serrated knife, carefully slice cake into even ½-inch slices. Lay the slices on a flat work surface and cut out cookies, staying away from the browned edges of the cake. Gently brush any loose crumbs from the cut edges of the cookies. Reserve and freeze the cake scraps for other uses.

2. Place a rack on a baking sheet with 1-inch sides. Put 1 cookie on the rack and coat with Corn Syrup Glaze (page 30). Repeat until all cookies have been cut and glazed. Let dry completely. Decorate by piping on royal icing dots and hearts if desired.

 Makes approximately 28 2-inch cookies.

Baby **R**attles

SEE THIS COOKIE IN PHOTO 7.

WORKING METHOD: Mix master recipe of icing to outline consistency. Divide icing into 5 bowls. Dilute with water-meringue powder mixture to desired consistencies (see pages 27–28). Tint with paste dye. Keep icing covered when you are not actually using it.

1. *For the base coat:*
   ICING CONSISTENCY: Base
   ICING COLOR: Light blue

Any shortbread or sugar cookie dough

Dab icing on the rattle with a spatula (Method I, pages 34–35) and spread to the edges of the cookie. Let dry completely. Reserve a small amount of icing for the waves.

2. **For the baby ducks and ornamentation:**
   ICING CONSISTENCY: Outline
   ICING COLOR: Pastel yellow

   Using a #2 tip, pipe on dots, lines, and curves to ornament the rattle. Using a #1 tip, pipe on the baby ducks.

3. **For the mother duck:**
   ICING CONSISTENCY: Base
   ICING COLOR: White

   Using a #1 tip, pipe on the mother duck. Let dry completely.

4. **For the waves:**
   Using a #1 tip and the reserved icing from step 1, pipe waves below the ducks.

5. **For the beaks:**
   ICING CONSISTENCY: Outline
   ICING COLOR: Gold

   Using a #1 tip, pipe beaks on all the ducks.

6. **For the eyes:**
   ICING CONSISTENCY: Outline
   ICING COLOR: Black

   Using a #1 tip, pipe eyes on the ducks. Let dry completely.

June

Cookie Crumbs— Baking in the Fast Lane

Usually you can successfully bake 2 sheets of cookies at the same time if you follow these simple steps:

1. Before you preheat the oven, arrange the baking racks to divide the oven into thirds.

2. Preheat the oven and place the sheets on the racks. Halfway through the baking period reverse the sheets top to bottom and front to back.

Suggested Cutters

Birthday cakes, simple geometric shapes, Easter shapes, anything for adult parties.

Chocolate Lovers' Shortbread, Mainlined with Espresso

*T*his sophisticated adult cookie, loaded with chocolate and jolted with a shot of espresso, is bittersweet, seductive, and smooth. Inspired by a Maida Heatter recipe that calls for home-ground coffee beans, this dough substitutes instant espresso powder, available in most grocery stores. I like it for "over-the-hill" birthday-cake cookies and for Easter bunnies, using chocolate-covered coffee beans to create the darker inner-ear areas.

3/4 cup (1 1/2 sticks) unsalted butter, room temperature

1 1/2 cups confectioners' sugar

3 cups bleached all-purpose flour

3/4 cup Dutch-process unsweetened cocoa powder

2 teaspoons instant espresso coffee powder

1/4 to 1/2 cup espresso, cold strong coffee, or water (optional)

---

1. Beat the butter in a large mixing bowl with an electric mixer on medium speed until light and fluffy, about 2 minutes. Add the sugar, flour, cocoa powder, and espresso powder. Continue to mix on high speed until the mixture is well combined and crumbly.

2. With your hands, try to knead the crumbs into a pliable dough. If the dough will not mass into a ball or if the ball looks cracked and dry, knead in dribbles of coffee, espresso, or water until the dough is pliable but not sticky.

3. Turn the dough onto a large piece of plastic wrap or place it in a reclosable plastic bag. Knead the dough several times, and form into a disk 2 inches thick. Refrigerate for 30 minutes.

4. Meanwhile, preheat the oven to 300° F. Line baking sheet(s) with parchment paper. Lightly dust the work surface and rolling pin with cocoa powder. Remove half the dough from the plastic; rewrap and refrigerate the remainder. Roll the dough to a thickness of $^1/_4$ inch and cut into shapes. With a spatula, transfer cookie cutouts to an ungreased baking sheet, keeping them at least 1 inch apart. Form scraps into a ball and chill. Roll and cut remaining dough and scraps.

5. Bake 25 minutes or until the cookies spring back when pressed lightly with your finger. Cool the cookies on the baking sheet for 5 minutes and then transfer them with a spatula to a rack to finish cooling.

 Makes approximately 3 dozen 3-inch cookies.

Birthday **C**akes

SEE THIS COOKIE ON THE FRONT COVER.

WORKING METHOD: Mix master recipe of icing to outline consistency. Divide icing into 10 bowls. Dilute with water-meringue powder mixture to the required consistencies (see pages 27–28). Tint with paste dye. Keep icing covered when you are not actually using it.

1. **For the cake stand:**
   ICING CONSISTENCY: Base
   ICING COLOR: White

   Apply base coat with a spatula (Method I, pages 34–35), gently spreading icing to the edges of the cake stand. Let dry to the touch.

continued on next page

Suggested Dough

Any shortbread, sugar cookie, or chocolate dough

Birthday Cakes (*cont.*)

2. *For the cake:*

ICING CONSISTENCY: Base
ICING COLOR: Pale blue or, for a more feminine look, pale pink

With a spatula dab icing in the middle of the cookie and spread gently to the edges. Let dry to the touch.

3. *For the candle glow:*

ICING CONSISTENCY: Base
ICING COLOR: Light yellow

Dab icing on the top part of the cookie and gently spread to the edges, leaving a bare space between the candle glow and the top of the cake. Let dry to the touch.

4. *For the handwritten greeting:*

ICING CONSISTENCY: Outline
ICING COLOR: Medium lavender

Using a #1 tip, write *Happy Birthday* on the lower part of the cookie. With a #2 tip, pipe a horizontal line to separate the cake stand from the cake. Reserve a small amount of lavender icing for the garland dots (step 5).

5. *To begin the cake garland:*

ICING CONSISTENCY: Outline
ICING COLOR: Medium blue or medium pink

Using a #2 tip, pipe on the remaining 2 horizontal lines at the bottom, making sure to leave at least $1/2$ inch between them.

Following directions for a cake garland (page 39) pipe on the first row of U shapes (called *swags*). Pipe on the lavender dots in the middle of each swag. Let dry to the touch.

Snowman,
Santa,
Miniature
Gingerbread
Men, Dreidels,
Miniature Bell,
Minisnowmen,
Snow-Covered
Cottage, and
Miniature
Candy Canes

3

Above: An Apple for the Teacher, Football, and Soccer Ball

At left: Bluebirds, Pansies, and Easter Eggs à la Fabergé

Above: Peter Rabbit Cookie, Pinto Pony, Scottie Dogs, Coyote, and Pig

At left: Ghost, Witch, Frankenstein Cookie, Black Cats,
Golden Leaves, and Pumpkins

6

Above: Autumn Leaves, Indian Corn, Acorns, and Holly Leaves

*At Right: Miniature Baby Bears, Pink Dotted Swiss Heart,
Heart with Swirls and Ruffles, Baby Rattle, Miniature
Baby Bears, and Wedding Cake*

7

Seagulls, Red-White-and-Blue Stars, Lighthouse, Statue of Liberty Cookie, and Lobster

6. **For the remainder of the cake garland, string-of-pearls garland, and candles:**
   ICING CONSISTENCY: Outline
   ICING COLOR: White

   Using a #2 tip, pipe on a white swag to finish the cake garland. Pipe on a horizontal string-of-pearls garland (see page 40) at the top of the cake. Pipe on candles, choosing different lengths to add dimension to the cookie. Let dry to the touch.

7. **For the flames:**
   ICING CONSISTENCY: Outline
   ICING COLOR: Gold

   Using a #2 tip, pipe a flame on each candle.

8. **For the flower buds:**
   ICING CONSISTENCY: Outline
   ICING COLOR: Pink

   Using a #2 tip, pipe flower buds (page 38) at the base of the cake. Let dry to the touch.

9. **For the bud accents:**
   ICING CONSISTENCY: Outline
   ICING COLOR: Red

   Using a #1 tip, pipe a dot of accent color at the tip of each bud.

10. **For the leaves:**
    ICING CONSISTENCY: Outline
    ICING COLOR: Leaf green

    Using a #1 tip, pipe leaves on each bud. Let all icing dry completely.

Flossie the Cow Cookies

WORKING METHOD: Mix master recipe of icing to outline consistency. Divide icing into 6 bowls. Dilute with water-meringue powder mixture to desired consistencies (see pages 27–28). Tint with paste dye. Keep icing covered when you are not actually using it.

Suggested Dough

Any dark dough, chocolate, or gingerbread

1. **For the background:**
   ICING CONSISTENCY: Base
   ICING COLOR: White

   Dab icing on the cow's body and spread with a spatula (Method I, pages 34–35), leaving holes for the spots. The spots should have gently irregular shapes. Do not ice the udder area. Let dry completely.

2. **For the brown spots:**
   ICING CONSISTENCY: Flow
   ICING COLOR: Dark brown

   Using a #2 or #3 tip, squeeze out icing to fill in the spots.

3. **For the udder:**
   ICING CONSISTENCY: Base
   ICING COLOR: Coral

   Using a #2 or #3 tip, pipe on the udder, making a shape like a script letter "M."

4. **For the stem of the flower bud garland:**
   ICING CONSISTENCY: Outline
   ICING COLOR: Leaf green

See page 38 for garland piping instructions. Using a #1 tip, pipe a long stem from the middle of the cow's chest up to the top of the back. Let dry to the touch. Reserve some icing for the leaves.

5. **For the flower buds:**
   ICING CONSISTENCY: Outline
   ICING COLOR: Coral

   Using #2 tip, pipe on flower buds. Let dry to the touch.

6. **For the leaves:**
   Using the icing reserved from the stem, with a #1 tip add green leaves to the buds. Let dry to the touch.

7. **For the bud tips:**
   ICING CONSISTENCY: Outline
   ICING COLOR: Red

   Using a #1 tip, dot the tip of each bud with a red accent. Let the cookies dry completely.

Bride's Bouquet Wedding Cookies

*T*his dough, the color of cream and studded with large pieces of rose petal, is undoubtedly the most elegantly beautiful in the book. The flavors of rose water and nutmeg marry well, suggesting an old-world spiciness with floral overtones.

   When I make these cookies for weddings, I cut and decorate them to look like wedding cakes, using petals from flowers in the bride's bouquet or the wedding decorations, if any of those flowers are edible and free of pesticides. The

continued on next page

flower girls pass around the cookies at the reception as favors for the guests to take home.

Rose water is available at drugstores, at specialty food shops, and by mail order. Consult a reliable herbal guide to guarantee that the flower petals are edible; do not use commercially grown flowers.

Line the baking sheets with parchment so that any pieces of petal accidentally touching the sheet will not burn or stick.

3 1/4 cups bleached all-purpose flour	1 cup butter
1/2 teaspoon salt	1 cup sugar
1/2 teaspoon cinnamon	3 large egg yolks
1/2 teaspoon freshly ground nutmeg	1/4 cup rose water
1/4 teaspoon mace	1 cup edible rose petals

1. In a small mixing bowl, combine the flour, salt, cinnamon, nutmeg, and mace. Stir to blend.

2. In a large mixing bowl, using a mixer, beat the butter and sugar until creamy. Add the egg yolks, 1 at a time, beating well after each.

3. With the mixer on medium-low, beat in the dry ingredients alternately with the rose water, beginning and ending with the dry ingredients and beating only enough to mix thoroughly.

4. Using a large wooden spoon, fold in the rose petals. Turn the dough onto a large piece of plastic wrap or place it in a reclosable plastic bag. Chill in the refrigerator for 30 minutes. Meanwhile, preheat the oven to 350° F.

5. Lightly flour the work surface and rolling pin and remove half of the dough from the plastic; rewrap and refrigerate the other half. Roll the dough to a thickness of 1/4 inch

and cut into shapes, pressing down hard on the cutter to cut cleanly through any pieces of rose petal. With a spatula, transfer cookie cutouts to a parchment-lined baking sheet, keeping them at least 1 inch apart. Form scraps into a ball and chill. Roll and cut remaining dough and scraps.

6. Bake 10–12 minutes or until light brown around the edges. Cool the cookies on the baking sheet for 5 minutes and then carefully remove them to a rack to cool completely.

 Makes approximately 2 dozen large cookies.

Wedding Cakes

SEE THIS COOKIE IN PHOTO 7.

WORKING METHOD: Mix master recipe of icing to outline consistency. Divide icing into 5 bowls. Dilute with water-meringue powder mixture to desired consistencies (see pages 27–28). Tint with paste dye. Keep icing covered when you are not actually using it.

1. *To ice the cake:*
    ICING CONSISTENCY: Base
    ICING COLOR: White

Dab icing on the cookie (Method I, pages 34–35) and spread gently to the edges. Let dry completely.

2. *For the horizontal lines:*
    ICING CONSISTENCY: Outline
    ICING COLOR: White

Using a #2 tip, pipe a horizontal line on the upper edge of each cake tier. Reserve enough white icing for the dots and garland drapery (technically called *swags*).

continued on next page

Suggested Dough

Any shortbread or sugar cookie dough

Wedding Cakes (*cont.*)

3. *For the white swags:*

For cake garland piping instructions, see page 39. Using the reserved white icing (step 2) and a #2 tip, pipe the first swag of the garland on each tier. Let dry to the touch.

4. *For the pink swags and flower buds:*

ICING CONSISTENCY: Outline
ICING COLOR: Light pink

Using a #2 tip, pipe the second swag on each tier. Let dry to the touch. Pipe a flower bud on each swag. Reserve enough icing for the flowers topping the cake.

5. *For the white dots:*

Using the reserved white outline icing (step 3) and a #2 tip, pipe dots below each swag.

6. *For the bud accents:*

ICING CONSISTENCY: Outline
ICING COLOR: Medium rose

Using a #1 tip, pipe an accent on the tip of each flower bud. Let dry to the touch. Reserve icing for the flowers on top of the cake.

7. *For the leaves:*

ICING CONSISTENCY: Outline
ICING COLOR: Moss green

Using a #1 tip, pipe leaves at the base of the flower buds. Reserve icing for the flowers on top of the cake.

8. *For the bouquet on top of the cake:*

Using the reserved icing from steps 4, 6, and 7, make flower buds in a random arrangement on the top of the cake. Let dry completely.

The Perfect Cookie for Summer Shortcakes

*T*hese shortbread cookies, blonde in complexion, delicate in texture, and not too sweet, marry perfectly with fresh-picked berries and whipped cream or (my favorite) berry sauces and chilled sabayon.

The cookies look beautiful decorated with royal-icing berries and vines. Since they keep well for at least a week, you can produce a last-minute, show-stopping dessert by sandwiching a filling between a decorated top cookie and a plain bottom one.

2 cups bleached all-purpose flour	1 cup (2 sticks) unsalted butter, cut into
1/2 cup confectioners' sugar	tablespoon-size chunks, kept chilled
1/4 teaspoon salt	3 tablespoons ice water

1. In a large bowl, combine the flour, sugar, and salt. Stir to blend. With a pastry blender, cut in the butter until it is the size of small peas. Add the ice water and, with a fork, stir to blend and form into a dough.

2. Preheat the oven to 350° F. Turn the dough onto a lightly floured surface and knead 3 or 4 times; if the dough is too sticky, refrigerate for 30 minutes before continuing. Shape into a disk about 1 inch thick. Roll to a thickness of 1/8 inch. Cut with a 3 1/2-inch round, fluted cookie cutter (or any cutter you choose).

3. With a spatula, transfer cookie cutouts to an ungreased baking sheet, keeping them

continued on next page

Cookie Crumbs—Chilled Lemon Sabayon

Unlike the classic sabayon (or its Italian cousin, zabaglione), which must be made at the last minute, this delicious lemony custard can be held in the refrigerator as long as 8 hours. Layer the sabayon between 2 cookies and spoon ripe, fresh berries alongside. You will need a glass or stainless steel double boiler.

Suggested Cutters

3 1/2-inch fluted round cutters for shortcakes.

The Perfect Cookie for Summer Shortcakes (*cont.*)

at least 1 inch apart. Form scraps into a ball and chill for 15 minutes. Roll and cut remaining dough and scraps.

4. Bake 15–20 minutes or until the edges are lightly browned. Cool the cookies on the baking sheet for 3 minutes, then transfer to a wire rack to cool completely.

 Makes approximately 16 round 3 1/2-inch cookies.

*L*emon *S*abayon

4 large egg yolks	1/2 cup (1 stick) salted butter at room temperature, cut into tablespoon-size pieces
4 large eggs	
1 cup fresh lemon juice	
3/4 cup superfine sugar	1/2 cup heavy whipping cream, whipped to soft peaks

1. Fill the bottom of the double boiler with water and bring to a simmer. When you put the boiler together, the top piece should be above the water level.

2. Remove the top of the boiler from the heat and add the egg yolks and eggs. Whisk to combine. Whisk in the sugar a little at a time. Whisk the egg-sugar mixture until it is light in color, about 3 minutes. Whisk in the lemon juice.

3. Replace top of the boiler and whisk the mixture continuously over the simmering water, until the sabayon becomes frothy and thick. Lift the whisk occasionally, letting the custard drip back into the pan. Remove from the heat just as soon as ribbons of custard start to form and trail from the whisk.

4. Whisk for another minute to cool; gently whisk in the butter a little at a time until thoroughly incorporated. Continue whisking until the sabayon is tepid. To help the custard set, place the top of the boiler with the tepid sabayon in a large bowl of ice and whisk periodically for about 10 minutes. Fold in the cream and refrigerate for at least 2 hours before serving.

Camp Cookies for a Crowd

*W*hen my children headed off to camp last summer, I sent them cookies (packed in popped popcorn) to relieve the pains of homesickness. My son, at a camp on the Oregon coast, received cookie whales, lobsters, crabs, lighthouses, shells, sailboats, fish, and other seaside treasures. My daughter, at a dude ranch, got cookie boots, horses, bison, coyotes, chili peppers, cacti, cowboys, and cowboy hats. This large recipe made enough to get 2 homesick campers through 4 weeks of camp.

---

12 tablespoons (1 ½ sticks) unsalted butter, room temperature

4 tablespoons vegetable shortening or vegetable oil

1 cup sugar

2 egg yolks

3 tablespoons half-and-half or light cream

1 ½ teaspoons vanilla extract

2 ½ cups bleached all-purpose flour

¼ teaspoon salt

¼ cup cornstarch

2 teaspoons baking powder

---

1. In a large bowl, using a mixer, beat the butter, shortening or oil, and sugar until creamy and light, about 3 minutes. Add the egg yolks, half-and-half or light cream, and vanilla extract. Beat until well combined, about 1 minute.

2. In a medium bowl, combine the flour, salt, cornstarch, and baking powder. Stir to mix well.

continued on next page

Cookie Crumbs— Cheap and Easy Packing Materials for Cookies

Depending on the size of the cookies you are packing, use egg cartons, empty yogurt containers with lids, clean quart-sized paper milk cartons, potato chip cans, or oatmeal boxes. Be sure to layer waxed paper between the cookies if they are stacked, to protect icing and cookies from cracking.

Suggested Cutters

Whales, flowers, suns, moons, lighthouses, sea shells, sea gulls, vegetables, or any summer motif.

Camp Cookies for a Crowd *(cont.)*

3. Add the flour mixture to the butter mixture and beat until it begins to blend and clump together, about 1 minute. Turn the dough onto a sheet of plastic wrap or place in a plastic bag and knead gently to shape into a soft dough, about 2 minutes.

4. Wrap the dough in the plastic or seal in the bag and refrigerate for at least 30 minutes but no longer than 2 hours. Meanwhile, preheat the oven to 350° F.

5. Lightly flour the work surface and rolling pin and remove half the dough from the plastic; rewrap and refrigerate the other half. Roll the dough to a thickness of $1/4$ inch and cut into shapes. With a spatula, transfer cookie cutouts to an ungreased baking sheet, keeping them at least 1 inch apart. Form scraps into a ball and chill for 15 minutes. Roll and cut remaining dough and scraps.

6. Bake 12–15 minutes or until lightly browned. Cool cookies on the baking sheet for 3 minutes; using a spatula, transfer to a rack to cool completely.

 Yield: Approximately 6 dozen 2-inch cookies.

Lighthouses

SEE THIS COOKIE IN PHOTO 8.

WORKING METHOD: Mix master recipe of icing to outline consistency. Divide icing into 5 bowls. Dilute icing with water-meringue powder mixture to desired consistencies (see pages 27–28). Tint with paste dye. Keep icing covered when you are not actually using it.

1. *For the base coat:*
   ICING CONSISTENCY: Base
   ICING COLOR: White

   Dab icing in the middle of the cookie and spread gently to the edges (Method I, pages 34–35), stopping short of the top. Let dry completely.

2. **For the building blocks:**
   ICING CONSISTENCY: Outline
   ICING COLOR: White

   Using a #2 tip, pipe on "mortar" to delineate the building blocks.

3. **For the roof and doors:**
   ICING CONSISTENCY: Base
   ICING COLOR: Black

   Using a #1 or #2 tip, carefully fill in the areas above and below the lantern, leaving space for the light. Pipe on the doors.

4. **For the light:**
   ICING CONSISTENCY: Base
   ICING COLOR: Medium yellow

   Using a #1 or #2 tip, fill in the light area. Let dry to the touch.

5. **For the gold beams:**
   ICING CONSISTENCY: Outline
   ICING COLOR: Gold

   Using a #1 tip, pipe on light beams. Using a tiny bit of icing, glue on a gold dragée for the lamp. Let dry completely.

Seagulls

SEE THESE COOKIES IN PHOTO 8.

WORKING METHOD: Mix master recipe of icing to outline consistency. Divide icing into 3 bowls. Dilute icing with water-meringue powder mixture to desired consistencies (see pages 27–28). Tint with paste dye. Keep icing covered when you are not actually using it.

1. For the base coat:
ICING CONSISTENCY: Base
ICING COLOR: White

Dab icing in the middle of the cookie and spread gently to the edges (Method I, pages 34–35), stopping short of the beak area.

2. For the beak:
ICING CONSISTENCY: Base
ICING COLOR: Yellow

Using a #1 tip, pipe on the beak. Let dry to the touch.

3. For the eye:
ICING CONSISTENCY: Outline
ICING COLOR: Black

Using a #1 tip, pipe on a small dot for the eye.

Pigs

SEE THIS COOKIE IN PHOTO 5 AND ON THE BACK COVER.

WORKING METHOD: Mix master recipe of icing to outline consistency. Divide icing into 3 bowls. Dilute icing with water-meringue powder mixture to desired consistencies (see pages 27–28). Tint with paste dye. Keep icing covered when you are not actually using it.

Suggested Dough

Any dough

1. *For the base coat:*
   ICING CONSISTENCY: Base
   ICING COLOR: Pink

   Dab icing in the middle of the cookie and spread gently to the edge (Method I, pages 34–35). Let dry to the touch.

2. *For the outlines:*
   ICING CONSISTENCY: Outline
   ICING COLOR: Pink

   Using a #2 tip, pipe the outline of the pig, giving definition to the ears, curly tail, snout, and jaw. Let dry to the touch.

3. *For the facial details:*
   ICING CONSISTENCY: Outline
   ICING COLOR: Brown

   Using a #1 tip, pipe on the eye, eyebrow, nostril, and mouth. Let dry to the touch.

4. *Optional shading:*
   For subtle shading, use a clean artist's brush to brush pink powdered dye along the backbone and leg and in the ears.

Cookie Crumbs— Creamy-Filled Sandwich Cookies

For a quick and tasty variation, try this luscious filling.

1 cup mascarpone cheese
2 tablespoons sugar
1 teaspoon vanilla

1. Combine cheese, sugar, and vanilla in a small mixing bowl; beat with a mixer until fluffy. Gently spread a cookie with 2 tablespoons of filling.
2. Top with another cookie and press together carefully.

Makes approximately 10 filled 3-inch cookies.

Sugar-Chocolate Dough for Ice-Cream Sandwiches and Filled Cookies

When school is out and the kids are restless, let them make cookies for ice-cream sandwiches. This dough is perfect for stamping or molding, both easy techniques for small children. It doesn't stick and needs no chilling, which saves time; the cookies are formed directly on the baking sheets, which simplifies cleanup. Once baked, the imprinted cookies can be left plain or glazed with melted semisweet chocolate, which will harden as it cools.

This dough can also be rolled and cut with cutters. Whether plain or filled, stamped, molded, or cut, these cookies are fun, easy, and delicious. Ceramic or glass molds or stamps are sold in kitchenware shops and by mail order.

1/2 cup (1 stick) unsalted butter, room temperature
3/4 cup sugar
1 large egg
1 tablespoon milk
1/4 teaspoon salt

1 teaspoon vanilla extract
2 cups bleached all-purpose flour
1/3 cup Dutch-process unsweetened cocoa (optional, for chocolate cookies)

---

1. Preheat the oven to 350° F. With a mixer, beat the butter, sugar, cocoa (if using), egg, milk, salt, and vanilla together until light and creamy, about 4 minutes.

2. Add the flour to the butter mixture and mix until thoroughly combined. Form the dough into a ball and knead by hand until the dough is pliable and smooth, about 1 minute.

3. If you are working with cookie cutters, lightly flour the work surface and rolling pin. Divide the dough into 2 equal parts; wrap and refrigerate 1 part. Roll the other half to a thickness of $1/4$ inch and cut into shapes. With a spatula, transfer cookie cutouts to an ungreased baking sheet, keeping them at least 1 inch apart. Form scraps into a ball and chill. Roll and cut remaining dough and scraps.

4. If you are working with stamps, divide the dough into 16–18 balls. Place 1 ball on an ungreased baking sheet and press down with the stamp until the dough is about $1/4$-inch thick. Repeat for remaining balls, keeping cookies at least 1 inch apart.

5. If you are working with molds, follow the manufacturer's directions for forming the cookies.

6. Bake in the preheated oven 12–15 minutes or until nicely browned around the edges. Cool the cookies on the baking sheet for 3 minutes and then transfer them with a spatula to cool completely.

7. For ice-cream sandwiches, spread $1/4$ cup softened ice cream on a completely cool cookie and top with another cookie. Wrap with plastic wrap and freeze immediately.

 Makes approximately 16–18 stamped cookies or 10 3- to 4-inch rounds for ice-cream sandwiches.

Suggested Cutters, Stamps, and Molds

Try a round 3-inch cutter with crinkled edges for ice-cream sandwiches. Any summer motif, any Christmas motif (to bake with children during the holiday season).

Pinto Ponies

SEE THIS COOKIE IN PHOTO 5.

WORKING METHOD: Mix master recipe of icing to outline consistency. Divide icing into 2 bowls. Dilute icing with water-meringue powder mixture to desired consistencies (see pages 27–28). Tint with paste dye. Keep icing covered when you are not actually using it.

1. *For the spots:*
ICING CONSISTENCY: Base
ICING COLOR: White

Using a spatula or a #2 tip (Method I, pages 34–35), spread or pipe irregular white markings on the pony. Don't forget the muzzle. Let dry completely.

2. *For the tail, mane, and eye:*
ICING CONSISTENCY: Outline
ICING COLOR: Black

Tint icing black. Using a #2 tip, pipe on tail, mane, and eye. Let dry completely.

Footballs

SEE THIS COOKIE IN PHOTO 3.

WORKING METHOD: Mix master recipe of icing to outline consistency. Divide icing into 3 bowls. Dilute icing with water-meringue powder mixture to desired consistencies (see pages 27–28). Tint with paste dye. Keep icing covered when you are not actually using it.

1. For the base coat:

ICING CONSISTENCY: Base
ICING COLOR: Brown

Dab icing in the middle of the cookie and spread gently to the edges (Method I, pages 34–35). Let dry to the touch.

2. For the lacing and lines:

ICING CONSISTENCY: Outline
ICING COLOR: White

Using a nonserrated ribbon tip, pipe white, slightly curved lines near each end of the football. With a #2 tip, pipe the lacing in the middle of the ball. Let dry to the touch.

3. For the seams:

ICING CONSISTENCY: Outline
ICING COLOR: Black

Using a #2 tip, pipe an oval around the lacing. Pipe on the remaining black seam lines. Let dry completely.

Soccer Balls

SEE THIS COOKIE IN PHOTO 3.

WORKING METHOD: Mix master recipe of icing to base consistency. Divide icing into 2 bowls. Adjust icing consistency with water-meringue powder mixture as needed (see pages 27–28). Tint with paste dye. Keep icing covered when you are not actually using it.

continued on next page

Suggested Dough

Any dough

Soccer Balls (*cont.*)

1. *For the base coat:*

ICING CONSISTENCY: Base
ICING COLOR: White

Dab icing in the middle of the cookie and spread gently to the edges (Method I, pages 34–35). Let dry completely.

2. *For the dark areas:*

ICING CONSISTENCY: Base
ICING COLOR: Black

Using a #2 tip, outline the ball. Pipe a pentagon (5-sided figure) in the middle of the cookie. Fill in the outlined pentagon with black icing. From each corner of the pentagon, pipe a line almost to the edge of the cookie. At the end of each line, outline a triangle. The triangles should be wider at the base than they are high. Using the #2 tip, fill in the triangles. Let dry completely.

*W*hole-*W*heat *T*eething *B*iscuits for *B*aby

ore, swollen gums can make babies cranky and unhappy. You can ease teething pains by giving the fretful baby frozen soft fruit or you can whip up a batch of homemade teething biscuits. While babies younger than 12 months should not eat honey, children older than that can safely enjoy these nutritious biscuits cut into any shape that a little hand can hold. I've cut them into tiny hands and feet, toy rattles, rabbits, and little trucks.

I suggest leaving them uniced, since young children shouldn't have a lot of sugar. If you want to give the biscuits as a gift, try putting a few in a clear or decorative cellophane bag and tying with a cascade of curly ribbon. These cook-

ies are so simple that a slightly older child can easily make them for a little brother or sister.

---

1 ½ cups whole-wheat flour

2 tablespoons soy flour

3 tablespoons nonfat dry-milk granules

2 tablespoons raw unprocessed bran or toasted wheat germ

¼ cup water

¼ cup honey

3 tablespoons molasses

2 large egg yolks

2 tablespoons oil

2 teaspoons vanilla extract

---

1. In a large mixing bowl, combine the flour, soy flour, dry-milk granules, and bran or wheat germ. Stir to blend.

2. In a small mixing bowl, combine the water, honey, molasses, egg yolks, oil, and vanilla extract. Whisk to blend thoroughly.

3. Add the water mixture to the dry mixture and stir until a dough is formed. If dry particles remain in the bottom of the bowl, sprinkle with water and stir until all the dry crumbs are incorporated and the dough forms a ball, completely leaving the sides of the bowl.

4. Preheat the oven to 350° F. Lightly grease 2 baking sheets or line with parchment paper. On a lightly floured surface, knead the dough until it is pliable, about 2 minutes. Form the dough into a disk and with a lightly floured rolling pin, roll the dough to a thickness of ¼ inch. Cut into desired shapes and, with a spatula, transfer the cut dough to the prepared baking sheets. Roll and cut the remaining dough and scraps.

5. Bake 15 minutes. Cool on the baking sheet for 2 minutes and then carefully transfer the cookies to a wire rack to cool completely.

 Makes approximately 2 dozen 4-inch teething biscuits.

Cookie Crumbs— Baby's First Birthday Gift

I like to give a year-old baby some new baby bottles decorated on the outside with bright, nontoxic, acrylic paints. I paint the baby's name and birth date on the bottle, and a few simple balloons, teddy bears, or zoo animals. Then I fill the bottles with teething biscuits cut into tiny teddy bears, ducks, or apples. If the baby's mother doesn't need the bottles right away, she can store them in the freezer, and use the biscuits as she needs them.

Suggested Cookie Cutters

Tiny hands and feet, rattles, little bears, miniature animals, fruit.

September

Cookie Crumbs—Sprinkles and Decorations from Your Spice Shelf

Your spice shelf probably holds some useful substitutes for commercial sprinkles. Do you need black sprinkles for Halloween cookies or sunflower centers? Try poppy seeds or ground espresso beans. Sprinkle sheep cookies with sesame seeds for a woolly look. Add rustic touches here and there with hulled raw sunflower seeds. To make the seeds stick, sprinkle the cookies while the royal icing is still damp.

Suggested Cutters

Suns, pumpkins, any birthday motif, carrots, any spring motif, school buses.

Cranberry-and-Citrus Sugar Cookies

Around the end of September when the new crop of oranges and dried cranberries begins appearing in the supermarket, I make these cookies. The pale yellow dough speckled with orange and red looks wonderful cut into pumpkins or melons, carrots or sunflowers.

Orange-flower water, imported from France, is available at cake-decorating stores and some gourmet shops. Or substitute the zest of half a grapefruit and 3 tablespoons of grapefruit juice for the orange zest and juice.

---

2 cups bleached all-purpose flour

1/2 teaspoon baking powder

1/4 teaspoon salt

1/2 cup (1 stick) unsalted butter

1 cup sugar

1 large egg

1 tablespoon orange-flower water (2 teaspoons orange juice plus 1/2 teaspoon orange extract can be substituted for the orange-flower water)

2 tablespoons freshly squeezed orange juice

Zest of 1 large orange, minced or grated (see page 14)

1/2 teaspoon vanilla extract

1/2 cup minced, dried cranberries

---

1. In a small mixing bowl, combine flour, baking powder, and salt. Stir to blend.

2. In a large mixing bowl, using an electric mixer, beat the butter and sugar until creamy, about 3 minutes. Beat in the egg, orange-flower water (or substitution), orange juice, orange zest, and vanilla extract until combined thoroughly.

3. With a wooden spoon, stir in the flour mixture and minced cranberries. Stir until all ingredients are well mixed and a pliable dough forms.

4. Wrap the dough in a large sheet of plastic wrap or place it in a reclosable plastic bag. Chill for 1 hour. Meanwhile, preheat the oven to 350° F.

5. Lightly flour the work surface and rolling pin. Remove half the dough from the plastic; rewrap and refrigerate the other half. Roll the dough to a thickness of $1/4$ inch and cut into shapes, pressing down hard to cut through any bits of cranberry. With a spatula, transfer the cookie cutouts to a lightly greased or parchment-lined baking sheet, keeping them at least 1 inch apart. Form scraps into a disk; roll and cut remaining dough and scraps.

6. Bake 10–12 minutes or just until the cookie springs back when the middle is touched lightly with a finger. Do not let the edges brown. Cool the cookies on the baking sheet for 3 minutes and then transfer them to a rack to cool completely.

 Makes approximately 2 dozen 3-inch cookies. This recipe can easily be doubled.

Pumpkins

SEE THESE COOKIES IN PHOTO 4.

WORKING METHOD: Mix master recipe of icing to outline consistency. Divide icing into 2 bowls. Dilute icing with water-meringue powder mixture to desired consistencies (see pages 27–28). Tint with paste dye. Keep icing covered when you are not actually using it.

1. *For the base coat:*
   ICING CONSISTENCY: Base
   ICING COLOR: Orange

continued on next page

Pumpkins (*cont.*)

Dab icing in the middle of the cookie and spread gently to the edges (Method I, pages 34–35). Let dry to the touch.

2. **For the outlines:**
ICING CONSISTENCY: Outline
ICING COLOR: Orange

Using a #2 tip, outline the pumpkin. Then pipe on curved lines suggesting the sections of the pumpkin. Let dry completely.

Chocolate Minichip Cookies

*R*olled and cut chocolate-chip cookies are a snap to make and easy to cut when you use mini-sized chocolate chips. Choose a sharp-edged cutter and be sure to cut firmly all the way through the dough and the chips. Use this dotted dough for cookie dogs, especially dalmatians.

1 cup (2 sticks) unsalted butter	1 large egg yolk
1/3 cup granulated sugar	2 1/2 cups bleached all-purpose flour
1/2 cup packed light-brown sugar	1 1/2 cups semisweet chocolate
2 teaspoons vanilla extract	minichips
1/2 teaspoon salt	

1. In a large mixing bowl, using an electric mixer, beat the butter, granulated sugar, brown sugar, vanilla, and salt until creamy. Beat in the egg yolk. Gradually add the flour and beat until thoroughly combined. By hand, stir in the chocolate chips.

Cookie Crumbs—
Cookie Crumble
Party Cake

Make your own premium mix-in ice cream by stirring crumbled, stale cookies into softened ice cream. Spread the ice cream between 2 cake layers and freeze it for a birthday party or other celebration. After the cake and ice cream are frozen solid (about 2 hours), decorate with your favorite butter-cream icing or glaze. Return to the freezer until just before serving.

2. Turn the dough onto a large piece of plastic wrap or place it in a reclosable plastic bag. Chill in the refrigerator for 30 minutes. Meanwhile, preheat the oven to 350° F.

3. Lightly flour the work surface and rolling pin and remove half the dough from the plastic; rewrap and refrigerate the other half. Roll the dough to a thickness of 1/4 inch and cut into shapes. With a spatula, transfer cookie cutouts to an ungreased baking sheet, keeping them at least 1 inch apart. Form scraps into a ball and chill. Roll and cut remaining dough and scraps.

4. Bake 10–12 minutes or until golden brown. Let the cookies cool on the baking sheet for 5 minutes and then carefully transfer the fragile cookies to a rack to cool completely. The cookies will harden and become firm enough to decorate as soon as the warm chocolate has cooled and hardened, about 30 minutes.

 Makes approximately 3 dozen 3-inch cookies. This recipe can easily be doubled.

Apples for the Teacher

SEE THIS COOKIE IN PHOTO 3.

WORKING METHOD: Mix master recipe of icing to outline consistency. Divide icing into 4 bowls. Dilute icing with water-meringue powder mixture to desired consistencies (see pages 27–28). Tint with paste dye. Keep icing covered when you are not actually using it.

1. *For the base coat:*
   ICING CONSISTENCY: Base
   ICING COLOR: Deep red

   Dab icing in the middle of the cookie and spread gently to the edges. (Method I, pages 34–35), stopping short of the stem and leaf areas. Let dry completely.

continued on next page

Suggested Cutters

Dogs, apples for the teacher, lunch boxes, Halloween motifs, leaves, pumpkins, or any autumn motif.

Suggested Dough

Any dough

Apples for the Teacher (*cont.*)

2. **For the leaves:**
   ICING CONSISTENCY: Base
   ICING COLOR: Leaf green

   Dab icing in the middle of the leaf area and spread gently to the red area of the apple and the cookie edge. Let dry to the touch.

3. **For the stem and central vein:**
   ICING CONSISTENCY: Outline
   ICING COLOR: Green, 1 or 2 shades lighter than leaves

   Using a #2 tip, pipe on the stem and outline the leaf. Pipe a line down the middle of the leaf to create the central vein.

4. **For the writing:**
   ICING CONSISTENCY: Outline
   ICING COLOR: White

   Using a #1 or #2 tip, pipe on the word *Teacher* in your best handwriting. Let dry completely.

October

Striped and Marbled Dough for Spooky Cookies

This pliable, easy-to-handle dough lends itself to marbling or striping. Try orange, white, and black for Halloween, or red, white, and blue for patriotic holidays. For cutters smaller than about 4 inches, make 6 alternately colored stripes of dough; for larger cutters, make three stripes, so that a stripe of each color will appear in each cookie. When you reroll the scraps, the dough will be marbled, so cut as many striped cookies as possible from the first rolling.

1 cup (2 sticks) salted butter	3 cups bleached all-purpose flour
1 cup sugar	3 tablespoons milk
1 large egg	1 teaspoon orange paste food coloring
1 teaspoon vanilla extract	1 teaspoon black paste food coloring
2 teaspoons baking powder	

1. Preheat the oven to 400° F. In a large bowl, using an electric mixer, beat the butter and sugar until creamy. Beat in the egg and vanilla extract.

2. In a small bowl combine the baking powder and flour. Stir to blend.

3. Gradually add the flour mixture to the butter mixture. Beat until well combined. Add the milk and beat until dough masses around the beaters, about 2 minutes.

4. Divide the dough into three equal portions. Leave one portion plain; set aside.

continued on next page

Cookie Crumbs— Baking Powder

Baking powder keeps its potency for about a year. Check the bottom of the can for the expiration date. In an emergency, you can make 1 tablespoon of a baking powder substitute satisfactory for most uses by mixing 1 teaspoon of baking soda with 2 teaspoons of cream of tartar.

Suggested Cookie Cutters

Autumn leaves, any Halloween or Thanksgiving motif, Fourth of July stars.

Striped and Marbled Dough for Spooky Cookies (*cont.*)

5. Add approximately 1 teaspoon orange paste food coloring to the second portion. With your hands knead the coloring into the dough until it becomes uniformly orange with no white streaks. Set aside. Repeat using black food coloring.

6. Lightly flour a nonstick work surface. Depending on the size cutters you choose, form the dough either into 3 logs approximately 10 inches long by 2 inches in diameter or into 6 logs, 2 of each color, approximately 10 inches long by 1 inch in diameter. Lay the logs next to each other and flatten lightly with your hands. Roll to a thickness of $1/3$ inch; you will have a sheet with 3 wide stripes or 6 narrower ones.

7. Cut into shapes. Stripes can run vertically, horizontally, or diagonally. With a spatula, transfer cutouts to an ungreased baking sheet, keeping them at least 2 inches apart. Form scraps into a ball and repeat, rolling and cutting the dough into marbled cookies.

8. Bake 10 minutes or until cookies spring back when pressed lightly with a finger. Let cookies cool on the baking sheet for 3 minutes and then carefully transfer to a rack to cool completely. Decorate as desired.

 Makes approximately 4 dozen 3-inch cookies.

Red-White-and-Blue Stars

SEE THESE COOKIES IN PHOTO 8.

WORKING METHOD: Mix master recipe of icing to outline consistency. Adjust consistency as needed with water-meringue powder mixture (see pages 27–28). Tint with paste dye. Keep icing covered when you are not actually using it.

1. **For the small stars:**
   ICING CONSISTENCY: Outline
   ICING COLOR: White

With a #2 or #3 tip, pipe icing into the middle of the star forming a smaller star. Let dry completely.

Black-Pepper Cookies

Extend greetings to your friends in the warmest way—with spiced pepper cookies. A touch of black pepper underlines the other flavors, making these cookies a favorite autumn treat. This dough needs to be well chilled, so mix the dough one day and make the cookies the next.

1 cup (2 sticks) unsalted butter	1 teaspoon ground ginger
1 cup sugar	1 teaspoon ground cinnamon
1 cup dark corn syrup	1 teaspoon ground cloves
1 tablespoon vinegar	1/2 teaspoon finely ground black pepper
4 1/2 cups bleached all-purpose flour	2 large eggs
1 teaspoon baking soda	

continued on next page

Black-Pepper Cookies (*cont.*)

1. In a heavy-bottomed saucepan over medium heat, melt the butter. Add the sugar, corn syrup, and vinegar. Bring the mixture to a low boil and immediately remove it from the heat. Cool to room temperature.

2. Meanwhile, in a medium bowl, add the flour, baking soda, ginger, cinnamon, cloves, and pepper. Stir to combine.

3. Beat the eggs into the butter-sugar mixture. Add the dry ingredients and stir until all ingredients are well combined and form a dough. Scrape the dough onto a large sheet of plastic wrap or place in a reclosable plastic bag. Seal the bag or tightly close the wrap and refrigerate dough for at least 2 hours, preferably overnight.

4. Preheat the oven to 375° F. Lightly flour the work surface and rolling pin; remove half the dough from the plastic; rewrap and refrigerate the other half. Roll the dough to a thickness of $1/4$ inch and cut into shapes. With a spatula, transfer cookie cutouts to an ungreased baking sheet, keeping them at least 2 inches apart. Form scraps into a ball and chill for 15 minutes. Roll and cut remaining dough and scraps.

5. Bake 10—12 minutes for soft cookies or 13-15 minutes for crisp cookies. Transfer soft cookies from the baking sheet to a wire rack immediately. Allow crisp cookies to cool completely on the baking sheet.

Makes approximately 5 dozen 3-inch cookies.

Cookie Crumbs— Too Soft or Too Hard?

Undecorated cookies that have become crisp from sitting out will soften if you store them for a day or so in a closed container with half an apple. Undecorated cookies that are too soft can be hardened by placing them on a baking sheet in a preheated 300• F oven. Turn off the oven and leave the cookies for several hours until they become crisp.

Suggested Cookie Cutters

Any cutters with autumn, Halloween, or Thanksgiving motifs.

Ghosts

SEE THIS COOKIE IN PHOTO 4.

WORKING METHOD: Mix master recipe of icing to outline consistency. Divide icing into 2 bowls. Dilute icing with water-meringue powder mixture to desired consistencies (see pages 27–28). Tint with paste dye. Keep icing covered when you are not actually using it.

1. **For the base coat:**
   ICING CONSISTENCY: Base
   ICING COLOR: White

   Dab icing in the middle of the cookie and spread gently to the edges (Method I, pages 34–35). Let dry completely.

2. **For the facial features:**
   ICING CONSISTENCY: Outline
   ICING COLOR: Black

   Using a #2 tip, pipe on the eyes and mouth. Let dry completely.

Suggested Dough

Gingerbread, chocolate, or spice

Witches

SEE THIS COOKIE IN PHOTO 4.

WORKING METHOD: Mix master recipe of icing to outline consistency. Divide icing into 6 bowls. Dilute icing with water-meringue powder mixture to desired consistencies (see pages 27–28). Tint with paste dye. Keep icing covered when you are not actually using it.

1. For the dress and hat:
ICING CONSISTENCY: Base
ICING COLOR: Black

Using a spatula, dab icing onto the dress and hat areas; spread gently to the edges (Method I, pages 34–35), stopping short of the face and neck. Let dry completely.

2. For the face:
ICING CONSISTENCY: Base
ICING COLOR: Light bluish green

Dab icing on the face area and gently spread to the edges. Let dry to the touch.

3. For the hair and warts:
ICING CONSISTENCY: Outline
ICING COLOR: Light bluish green

Using a #2 tip, pipe on the hair and the warts on nose and chin. Let dry to the touch.

4. For the eye:
ICING CONSISTENCY: Outline
ICING COLOR: Yellow

Using a #2 tip, pipe on the eye. Let dry to the touch.

Suggested Dough

Gingerbread, chocolate, or spice

5. *For the accent lines:*
ICING CONSISTENCY: Outline
ICING COLOR: Black

Using a #1 tip, pipe on the pupil of the eye and accent lines for the hair, mouth, and warts. Let dry to the touch.

6. *For the hat band:*
ICING CONSISTENCY: Outline
ICING COLOR: Orange

With a small nonserrated ribbon tip, pipe on the hat band. Let dry completely.

Frankenstein Cookies

SEE FRANKENSTEIN IN PHOTO 4.

WORKING METHOD: Mix master recipe of icing to outline consistency. Divide icing into 8 bowls. Dilute icing with water-meringue powder mixture to desired consistencies (see pages 27–28). Tint with paste dye. Keep icing covered when you are not actually using it.

1. *For the pants and boots:*
ICING CONSISTENCY: Base
ICING COLOR: Black

With a spatula, dab icing on the bottom part of the cookie (Method I, pages 34–35); spread gently to the edges, forming the pants and boots, being sure to leave a space between the boot heel and the rest of the foot. Or, using a #2 tip (with base consistency icing), pipe on the outline of the pants and boots and fill in (Method II, pages 35–36). Let dry completely.

continued on next page

Suggested Dough

Gingerbread, chocolate, or spice

Frankenstein Cookies (*cont.*)

2. *For the shirt:*

ICING CONSISTENCY: Base
ICING COLOR: Light blue or gray

With a spatula, dab icing in the middle of the shirt area and spread gently to the edges, forming a V-necked shirt, stopping short of the hands. Let dry to the touch. Reserve a small amount of icing for the nose.

3. *For the head and ears:*

ICING CONSISTENCY: Base
ICING COLOR: Light green

With a spatula, dab icing in the middle of the head and spread gently to the edges. Let dry to the touch. Using a #1 tip, outline the ears.

4. *For the striped undershirt, hands, and eyes:*

ICING CONSISTENCY: Outline
ICING COLORS: White and red

Prepare a small decorating bag with a #1 or #2 tip; fill it with white icing. Fit a #1 or #2 tip into another small decorating bag and fill it with red icing. Pipe alternate lines of red and white into the V-neck area of the shirt. Using a #2 tip, fill in the hands with white icing. Using a #1 tip, pipe on white eyes. Let dry to the touch.

5. *For the hair:*

ICING CONSISTENCY: Outline
ICING COLOR: Orange

With a #1 or #2 tip, pipe on hair. Let dry to the touch.

6. *For the scars, facial features, collar, and buttons:*

ICING CONSISTENCY: Outline
ICING COLOR: Black

With a #2 tip, carefully pipe on the shirt collar and the buttons. Attach silver dragées, which represent the bolts in the neck, to the wet collar icing. Using a #1 tip, pipe on the mouth and the scars on cheek and forehead. Pipe on the pupils of the eye.

7. *For the nose:*

Using the reserved blue icing (step 2) and a #1 tip, pipe on the nose.

8. *For the brows and circles around the eyes:*

ICING CONSISTENCY: Outline
ICING COLOR: Green

Using a #1 tip, draw circles around the eyes and form eyebrows. Let dry completely.

Suggested Dough

Gingerbread, chocolate, or spice

Black **C**ats

SEE THESE COOKIES IN PHOTO 4.

WORKING METHOD: Mix master recipe of icing to outline consistency. Divide icing into 2 bowls. Dilute icing with water-meringue powder mixture to desired consistencies (see pages 27–28). Tint with paste dye. Keep icing covered when you are not actually using it.

1. For the base coat:
   ICING CONSISTENCY: Base
   ICING COLOR: Black

   Dab icing in the middle of the cookie and spread gently to the edges (Method I, pages 34–35). Let dry to the touch.

2. For the eyes:
   ICING CONSISTENCY: Outline
   ICING COLOR: Orange

   Using a #2 tip, pipe on eyes. Let dry completely.

Fresh Ginger Gingerbread Cookies

I always try to use fresh spices, whether I am baking or cooking savory dishes, and fresh ginger is one of my favorites. Peeled ginger root is easy to grate on the medium holes of a stainless steel grater or on a porcelain ginger grater, sold by some specialty food stores.

While the dough is chilling, bake a test cookie and taste it to make sure it is gingery enough. Baking will slightly subdue the ginger, so add more to the dough if you want more bite.

4 1/2 cups bleached all-purpose flour	2 teaspoons peeled, freshly grated ginger
1 1/2 teaspoons baking soda	1 teaspoon ground ginger
3/4 teaspoon baking powder	1 1/2 teaspoons cinnamon
1 cup (2 sticks) unsalted butter	1/2 teaspoon ground cloves
3/4 cup packed light-brown sugar	2 teaspoons salt
2 large eggs	1 cup dark, mild molasses

1. In a medium bowl, combine the flour, baking soda, and baking powder. Stir to blend.

2. In a large mixing bowl, using an electric mixer, cream the butter and sugar until light. Add the eggs, gingers, cinnamon, cloves, salt, and molasses, and beat well.

3. Add the flour mixture to the butter mixture and mix well. Scrape the dough into a re-closable plastic bag. Seal and chill dough for at least 2 hours.

continued on next page

Cookie Crumbs— Old-World Ginger Dough

If you really like the taste of ginger, make this dough into an Old-World Ginger Dough by adding crystallized ginger. Add about 1/3 cup hand-minced crystallized ginger to the dough. When you cut the cookies, remember to push down firmly to cut cleanly through the pieces of ginger.

Suggested Cutters

Any motif suggesting fall, Thanksgiving, or Christmas. This dough is too soft for making tree ornaments; instead use Gingerbread Dough for Ornaments (page 126).

Fresh Ginger Gingerbread Cookies (*cont.*)

4. Preheat the oven to 350° F. Flour the work surface and rolling pin, and remove half the dough from the plastic bag; rewrap and refrigerate the other half. Roll the dough to a thickness of ¹/₄ inch and cut into shapes. With a spatula, transfer cookie cutouts to an ungreased baking sheet, keeping them at least 1 inch apart. Form scraps into a ball and chill for 15 minutes. Roll and cut the remaining dough and scraps.

5. Bake 8–12 minutes or until the bottoms are barely browned. Let the cookies cool on the baking sheet for 5 minutes and then transfer them with a spatula to a rack to finish cooling.

 Makes approximately 4 dozen 3-inch cookies. This recipe can easily be doubled.

Coyotes

SEE THIS COOKIE IN PHOTO 5.

WORKING METHOD: Mix master recipe of icing to outline consistency. Divide icing into 5 bowls. Dilute icing with water-meringue powder mixture to desired consistencies (see pages 27–28). Tint with paste dye. Keep icing covered when you are not actually using it.

1. *For the base coat:*
   ICING CONSISTENCY: Base
   ICING COLOR: Southwest-adobe peach

   Using a spatula, dab icing in the middle of the cookie and spread gently to the edge (Method I, pages 34–35). Let dry to the touch.

2. **For the bandanna:**
   ICING CONSISTENCY: Base
   ICING COLOR: Light blue

   Using a spatula or #2 tip, spread or pipe on the bandanna. Let dry to the touch.

3. **For the blue fringe:**
   ICING CONSISTENCY: Outline
   ICING COLOR: Medium blue

   Using a #2 tip, pipe fringe in the middle of the bandanna and along the edge, leaving space on the edge for the white fringe. Let dry to the touch.

4. **For the white fringe:**
   ICING CONSISTENCY: Outline
   ICING COLOR: White

   Using a #2 tip, pipe on white fringe along the edge of the bandanna.

5. **For the eyes and toenails:**
   ICING CONSISTENCY: Outline
   ICING COLOR: Brown

   Using a #1 tip, pipe on toenails and a closed eyelid with eyelashes. Let dry completely.

Miniature Gingerbread Men

SEE THESE COOKIES IN PHOTO I.

WORKING METHOD: Mix master recipe of icing to outline consistency. Divide icing into 2 bowls. If necessary, adjust consistency with water-meringue powder mixture (see pages 27–28). Tint with paste dye. Keep icing covered when you are not actually using it.

1. For the eyes, mouth, and buttons:

ICING CONSISTENCY: Outline
ICING COLOR: White

Using a #1 tip, pipe on eyes, mouth, and, buttons. For medium or large gingerbread people, use a #2 tip.

2. For the bow ties:

ICING CONSISTENCY: Outline
ICING COLOR: Red

Using a #1 tip (or a #2 tip for larger gingerbread men), pipe on bow tie. Let dry completely.

Suggested Dough

Gingerbread

Spiced Molasses Cookies

Start the winter baking season off right by baking a batch of these buttery cookies for Thanksgiving. They are tender yet hold their shape, an excellent choice for shipping.

1 cup (2 sticks) unsalted butter, room temperature	5 cups bleached all-purpose flour
1 cup packed light brown sugar	1 tablespoon ground ginger
2 large eggs	2 teaspoons baking soda
2/3 cup molasses	1 teaspoon ground cinnamon
2 teaspoons vanilla extract	1/2 teaspoon salt
	1/4 teaspoon ground nutmeg

1. In a large bowl, using a mixer, beat the butter and sugar until light in color and creamy. Add the eggs one at a time, beating well after each. Beat in the molasses and vanilla extract until thoroughly combined.

2. In a medium bowl, add the flour, ginger, baking soda, cinnamon, salt, and nutmeg. Stir to blend.

3. Add the flour mixture to the butter mixture a little at a time and beat well. Scrape the dough into a reclosable plastic bag. Seal and chill the dough for 1 to 2 hours.

4. Preheat the oven to 350° F. Flour the work surface and rolling pin. Remove half the dough from the plastic bag; rewrap and refrigerate the other half. Roll the dough to a thickness of 1/4 inch and cut into shapes. With a spatula, transfer cookie cutouts to a lightly greased or parchment-lined baking sheet, keeping them at least 2 inches apart. Form scraps into a ball and chill for 15 minutes. Roll and cut remaining dough and scraps.

continued on next page

Cookie Crumbs— Smoothing Off Rough Edges

Sometimes cookies emerge from the oven with ragged edges either because the cutter was dull or because bits of fruit have poked through during baking. For perfect edges, file off the rough spots with an inexpensive fingernail file reserved for this purpose.

Suggested Cutters

Any cutter with an autumn, Thanksgiving, or Christmas theme.

Spiced Molasses Cookies (*cont.*)

5. Bake 10–15 minutes or until the bottoms are lightly browned. Cool the cookies on the baking sheet for 3 minutes and then transfer to a rack to cool completely.

 Makes approximately 5 dozen 3-inch cookies.

Autumn **L**eaves

SEE THESE COOKIES IN PHOTO **6.**

WORKING METHOD: Mix master recipe of icing to outline consistency. Divide icing into 4 bowls. Dilute icing with water-meringue powder mixture to desired consistencies (see pages 27–28). Tint with paste dye. Keep icing covered when you are not actually using it.

1. **For the base coat:**
   ICING CONSISTENCY: Base
   ICING COLORS: At least 3 autumn colors: garnet red, gold, green, or yellow

Choose one color for the base coat. Dab icing in the middle of the cookie and spread gently to the edges (Method III, page 36). While the icing is still wet, use a spatula to add dots of icing in an attractively contrasting color and swirl it into the base icing. Toothpicks work well for creating small veins of color. Let dry to the touch.

2. **For the outline and veins:**
   ICING CONSISTENCY: Outline
   ICING COLOR: One of the fall colors used as base coat

Using a #2 tip, outline the leaf and pipe on veins. Let dry completely.

Acorns

SEE THESE COOKIES IN PHOTO **6**.

WORKING METHOD: Mix master recipe of icing to outline consistency. Divide icing into 3 bowls. Dilute icing with water-meringue powder mixture to desired consistencies (see pages 27–28). Tint with paste dye. Keep icing covered when you are not actually using it.

1. **For the base coat:**
ICING CONSISTENCY: Base
ICING COLOR: Light brown.

Dab icing in the middle of the acorn and gently spread to the edges (Method I, pages 34–35), avoiding the area where the cap will be. Let dry to the touch.

2. **For the cap:**
ICING CONSISTENCY: Base
ICING COLOR: Dark brown

Dab icing on the top of the cookie to form the cap; spread gently to the edges. Let dry to the touch.

3. **For the details:**
ICING CONSISTENCY: Outline
ICING COLOR: Light brown

Using a #2 tip, pipe a continuous U-shaped pattern across the cap forming scales. Pipe a short line at the bottom of the cookie to form the acorn tip.

Suggested Dough

Chocolate, spice, or gingerbread

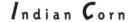 Indian Corn

SEE THIS COOKIE IN PHOTO 6.

WORKING METHOD: Mix master recipe of icing to outline consistency. Divide icing into 6 or 7 bowls. Dilute icing with water-meringue powder mixture to desired consistencies (see pages 27–28). Tint with paste dye. Keep icing covered when you are not actually using it.

Suggested Dough

Chocolate, spice, or gingerbread

1. **For the base coat:**
ICING CONSISTENCY: Base
ICING COLOR: Pale to medium yellow

Dab icing in the middle of the cookie and spread gently, stopping short of the area where the husk will be (Method I, pages 34–35). Let dry to the touch.

2. **For the husk:**
ICING CONSISTENCY: Base
ICING COLOR: Tan

Dab icing in the husk area and spread gently to the edges. Let dry to the touch.

3. For the leaves:
ICING CONSISTENCY: Outline
ICING COLOR: Tan, slightly darker than the husk

Using a #2 tip, pipe on lines to define the separate leaves of the husk. Let dry completely.

4. **For the kernels:**
ICING CONSISTENCY: Outline
ICING COLORS: Several colors to suggest kernels: yellow, orange, deep red, and black.

Using a #2 tip, pipe small, elongated kernels in straight lines, alternating colors several times. Using a #1 tip, pipe 1 or 2 black wiggly lines between the rows to show dried corn silk. Let dry completely.

Golden Leaves

SEE THESE COOKIES IN PHOTO 4.

WORKING METHOD: Mix master recipe of icing to outline consistency. Divide icing into 2 bowls. Dilute icing with water-meringue powder mixture to desired consistencies (see pages 27–28). Tint with paste dye. Keep icing covered when you are not actually using it.

1. **For the base coat:**
ICING CONSISTENCY: Base
ICING COLOR: Golden yellow

Dab icing in the middle of the cookie and spread gently to the edges (Method 1, pages 34–35). Let dry to the touch.

2. **For the outlines:**
ICING CONSISTENCY: Outline
ICING COLOR: Golden yellow

Using a #2 tip, outline the cookie. Pipe a line from the base of the leaf two-thirds of the way up the midline, forming the central vein. Let dry completely.

Suggested Dough

Gingerbread, chocolate, or spice

December

Cookie Crumbs—
Storing Cookies
for 6 Months or
Longer

Cookies that will be stored
from season to season need
special attention.

1. Choose a lean dough,
preferably one with veg-
etable shortening rather
than unsalted butter, which
has a shorter shelf life.
2. Layer the cookies between
sheets of waxed paper and
place in metal, cardboard, or
glass (not plastic) containers
with tight-fitting lids that
will keep out insects.
3. Store in a darkened area
at a constant room temperature (not in the attic) away
from fluorescent lights,
which may bleach the color
from royal icing.
4. Periodically check the
stored cookies for insects.
Several days before you
want to use the cookies,
check them again and make

Gingerbread Dough for Cookie Ornaments

Cookies used as ornaments must be crisp but not brittle, and hold their shape perfectly in the oven. They should be at least 1/4-inch thick. This dough meets all the criteria, producing cookies that are as delicious to eat as they are delightful to behold.

3 cups bleached all-purpose flour	1/2 cup unsalted butter
1 teaspoon baking soda	1/2 cup packed light-brown sugar
1 teaspoon ground cinnamon	1/2 cup maple-flavor syrup (or 1/4 cup
1 teaspoon ground ginger	maple-flavor syrup plus 1/4 cup
1 teaspoon ground allspice	molasses)
1 teaspoon ground cloves	1 large egg
1/2 teaspoon salt	

1. In a medium mixing bowl, combine 2 cups of the flour, the baking soda, cinnamon, ginger, allspice, cloves, and salt. Stir to blend.

2. In a large mixing bowl, using a mixer, beat the butter, brown sugar, and syrup or syrup-molasses mixture until creamy. Add the egg and beat until fluffy, about 2 minutes longer.

3. Gradually add the flour mixture and mix until thoroughly combined, about 3 minutes. Using a heavy wooden spoon, stir in the remaining 1 cup of flour until a pliable dough forms.

4. Turn the dough onto a large piece of plastic wrap or place it in a reclosable plastic bag. Chill for 15 minutes. Preheat the oven to 350° F.

5. Lightly flour the work surface and rolling pin. Remove half the dough from the plastic; rewrap and refrigerate the other half. Roll the dough to a thickness of ¼ inch and cut into shapes. With a spatula, transfer cookie cutouts to a lightly greased or parchment-lined baking sheet, keeping them at least 1 inch apart. Form scraps into a ball. Roll and cut remaining dough and scraps.

6. Bake 15–20 minutes or until golden brown. Cool the cookies on the baking sheet for 2 minutes and then transfer to a rack to cool completely.

 Makes approximately 2 dozen 4-inch ornament cookies. This recipe can easily be doubled.

Santas

SEE SANTA IN PHOTO 1 AND ON THE FRONT COVER.

WORKING METHOD: Mix master recipe of icing to outline consistency. Divide icing into 11 bowls. Dilute icing with water-meringue powder mixture to desired consistencies (see pages 27–28). Tint with paste dye. Keep icing covered when you are not actually using it.

1. *To outline the fur:*
   ICING CONSISTENCY: Outline
   ICING COLOR: White

   Most of the white fur areas are created by outlining and piping (Method II, pages 35–36). Using a #2 tip, pipe on the fur outlines at the bottom of Santa's coat, hat, sleeve cuff, and beard. Add eyebrows. Let dry to the touch.

continued on next page

---

repairs: The icing may have chipped or the dragées fallen off. Although no longer edible, they should be usable as ornaments.

Suggested Cutters

Anything with a Christmas or fall holiday theme.

Suggested Dough

Gingerbread

Santas (*cont.*)

2. To fill in the fur outlines:
ICING CONSISTENCY: Flow
ICING COLOR: White

Using a #1 tip, pipe in the outlined areas with the flow icing, moving the icing bag back and forth as you work. Let dry completely.

3. For the bag, pompon, and boot trim:
ICING CONSISTENCY: Base
ICING COLOR: White

Using a small spatula, dab icing on Santa's back and gently spread to form the bag. Dab on the pompon at the peak of the hat. Spread a rectangular strip at the ankle for the fur trim of the boot. Let dry completely.

4. For the coat, pants, and hat:
ICING CONSISTENCY: Base
ICING COLOR: Red

Gently spread dabs of icing to cover the coat, pants, and hat. Let dry completely.

5. For the boots and glove:
ICING CONSISTENCY: Base
ICING COLOR: Black

Using a #2 tip or a spatula, pipe or spread on Santa's boots and glove. Let dry completely.

6. For the belt:
ICING CONSISTENCY: Base
ICING COLOR: Holly green

Using a nonserrated ribbon tip, pipe on Santa's belt. Let dry to the touch.

7. **For the belt buckle:**
   ICING CONSISTENCY: Outline
   ICING COLOR: Gold

   Using a #1 tip, pipe on the belt buckle.

8. **For the flower buds and cheeks:**
   ICING CONSISTENCY: Outline
   ICING COLOR: Pink

   Using a #1 or #2 tip, pipe flower buds (see page 38) on the fur at the bottom of Santa's coat and hat, and dots for his cheeks.

9. **For the bud leaves:**
   ICING CONSISTENCY: Outline
   ICING COLOR: Leaf green

   Using a #1 tip, pipe leaves on the flower buds.

10. **For the nose and red accents:**
    ICING CONSISTENCY: Outline
    ICING COLOR: Red

    Using a #1 tip, pipe on the flower bud tips, dots on Santa's bag, his cherry nose, and a horizontal stripe through his boot fur.

11. **For the eyes:**
    ICING CONSISTENCY: Outline
    ICING COLOR: Light blue

    Using a #1 tip, pipe on Santa's eyes. Let dry completely.

Suggested Dough
———
Gingerbread

Miniature Candy Canes

SEE THESE COOKIES IN PHOTO I.

WORKING METHOD: Mix master recipe of icing to outline consistency. Divide icing into 2 bowls. Dilute icing with water-meringue powder mixture to desired consistencies (see pages 27–28). Tint with paste dye. Keep icing covered when you are not actually using it.

1. **For the base coat:**
ICING CONSISTENCY: Base
ICING COLOR: White

Apply dabs of icing with a spatula and gently spread to the edges (Method I, pages 34–35). Let dry completely.

2. **For the stripes:**
ICING CONSISTENCY: Outline
ICING COLOR: Red

Using a #1 or #2 tip, pipe diagonal stripes across the cane. Let dry completely.

Snow-Covered Cottages

SEE THIS COOKIE IN PHOTO I.

WORKING METHOD: Mix master recipe of icing to outline consistency. Divide icing into 3 bowls. Dilute icing with water-meringue powder mixture to desired consistencies (see pages 27–28). Tint with paste dye. Keep icing covered when you are not actually using it.

Suggested Dough
———
Gingerbread

1. For the snow:

ICING CONSISTENCY: Outline
ICING COLOR: White

Using a #2 tip, pipe snow on the roof. With a #1 tip, pipe on the snowy window. Let dry completely. Reserve a small amount of icing for the doorknob.

2. For the door and chimney:

ICING CONSISTENCY: Outline
ICING COLOR: Red

Tint icing red. Using a #2 tip, pipe on the door and chimney.

3. For the shutters:

ICING CONSISTENCY: Outline
ICING COLOR: Green

Using a #1 tip, pipe on shutters. Let dry completely

4. For the doorknob:

Using the reserved white icing, pipe on the doorknob.

Miniature Bells

SEE THIS COOKIE IN PHOTO 1.

WORKING METHOD: Mix master recipe of icing to outline consistency. Divide icing into 3 bowls. Dilute icing with water-meringue powder mixture to desired consistencies (see pages 27–28). Tint with paste dye. Keep icing covered when you are not actually using it.

continued on next page

Suggested Dough

Gingerbread

Miniature Bells (*cont.*)

1. *For the base coat:*
ICING CONSISTENCY: Base
ICING COLOR: White

Apply dabs of icing with a spatula and gently spread to the edges (Method I, pages 34–35). Let dry completely.

2. *For the holly berry and clapper:*
ICING CONSISTENCY: Outline
ICING COLOR: Red

With a #1 tip, pipe on one small holly berry. Pipe on a slightly larger red dot for the clapper.

3. *For the holly leaf:*
ICING CONSISTENCY: Outline
ICING COLOR: Green

With a #1 tip, pipe on a holly leaf. Let dry completely.

Suggested Dough

Gingerbread, sugar cookie, or shortbread

Dreidels

SEE THESE COOKIES IN PHOTO I.

WORKING METHOD: Mix master recipe of icing to outline consistency. Divide icing into 3 bowls. Dilute icing with water-meringue powder mixture to desired consistencies (see pages 27–28). Tint with paste dye. Keep icing covered when you are not actually using it. Apply dragées while icing is still wet.

1. **For the base coat:**
   ICING CONSISTENCY: Base
   ICING COLOR: White

   Apply dabs of icing with a spatula and gently spread to the edges (Method I, pages 34–35). Let dry completely.

2. **For the lettering:**
   ICING CONSISTENCY: Outline
   ICING COLOR: Light blue

   With a #2 tip, pipe on the Hebrew letters *nun, gimel, he,* or *shin.* Pipe a horizontal line at the top of the dreidel and a small curve around the base of the handle. Pipe a blue dot at the bottom. Before the icing dries, apply gold dragées at the points of the Hebrew letters. Let dry completely.

3. **For the gold accents:**
   In a small bowl, mix 1 teaspoon lemon extract with 1/8 teaspoon Luster Dust (see page 11), preferably Old Gold. Using a clean, small paint brush with a pointed tip, paint the gold finish on the handle and around the Hebrew letter. Let dry completely.

Chocolate Sugar Cookies for Ornaments

Children adore these cookies. They love the feel of the dough; they love rolling it out and cutting it into plain and fancy shapes. But most of all, they love decorating the ornaments with royal icing and scattering colored sprinkles and sugars on them.

Young children can string ribbons through the cookies to make either individual ornaments or cookie garlands, but an adult should probably drill

continued on next page

Cookie Crumbs— The Best Dough Temperature

When it comes to rolling dough, temperature is crucial—the temperature in the kitchen, the temperature of the dough, and the temperature of your hands. All 3

continued on next page

the holes (*page 136*). *Stored in a cool, dry place these cookies will last at least 2 months, so you can bake well ahead of time.*

Use this dough if your tree is green; if you have a white-flocked tree, make ornaments with Buttery Shortcookie Dough (page 136).

1. In a small mixing bowl, combine the sifted flour, baking powder, and salt. Stir to blend.

2. In a large mixing bowl, using an electric mixer, beat the shortening, butter, sugar, and vanilla extract until creamy. Beat in the eggs and chocolate until thoroughly combined.

3. Gradually add the flour mixture and beat until ingredients are thoroughly combined and the large crumbly pieces mass into a dough, about 2 minutes.

4. Wrap the dough in a large piece of plastic wrap or place it in a reclosable plastic bag. Refrigerate for 1 hour. Meanwhile, preheat the oven to 375° F.

5. Lightly flour the work surface and rolling pin. Remove half the dough from the plastic, making sure to rewrap; refrigerate the other half. Roll the dough to a thickness of ¹/₄ inch and cut into shapes. With a spatula, transfer cookie cutouts to a lightly greased or parchment-lined baking sheet, keeping them at least 1 inch apart. Form scraps into a ball and chill. Roll and cut remaining dough and scraps.

Cookie Crumbs (cont.)

should be as cool as possible to ensure that the dough is not too sticky to roll easily.

Chill the dough in the refrigerator. Don't think for a minute that you can hurry the process by putting the dough in the freezer: Either the outside will be cool, but the interior still warm; or, if you leave it too long, the inside will be cool, but the outside frozen and dried out.

Chill the dough until firm but not hard; if it is too cold and hard, it will crack, split, and be difficult to roll, especially if it contains a lot of butter. Its optimal temperature for rolling is about 72° F; it should yield slightly when pressed but not stick to your fingers.

Suggested Cutters

Any Christmas or Halloween motif.

6. Bake 10–12 minutes or until golden brown. Cool the cookies on the baking sheet for 5 minutes and then carefully transfer them to a rack to cool completely.

 Makes approximately 5 dozen 3-inch cookies.

Holly Leaves

SEE THESE COOKIES IN PHOTO 6.

WORKING METHOD: Mix master recipe of icing to outline consistency. Divide icing into 3 bowls. Dilute icing with water-meringue powder mixture to desired consistencies (see pages 27–28). Tint with paste dye. Keep icing covered when you are not actually using it.

Suggested Dough
_____

Chocolate, spice, or gingerbread

1. **For the base coat:**
   ICING CONSISTENCY: Base
   ICING COLOR: Medium green

   Dab icing in the middle of the cookie and spread gently to the edges (Method 1, pages 34–35). Before the base coat dries, proceed with the next step.

2. **For the outline and central vein:**
   ICING CONSISTENCY: Base
   ICING COLOR: Dark green

   Using a #2 tip, outline the cookie and pipe a large vein down the middle. Let dry to the touch.

3. **For the berries:**
   ICING CONSISTENCY: Outline
   ICING COLOR: Berry red

   Using a #2 tip, pipe on 3 dots in a triangular shape near the leaf base. Let dry completely.

Buttery Shortcookie Dough for Ornaments

**Cookie Crumbs—
To Hang Cookie
Ornaments**

Drill neat, round holes in the
cookies for ribbon hangers
using an electric drill fitted
with a small, clean bit. For
oversized ornaments, try
ribbon with stiffened wire
edges; it makes bows that
hold their shape perfectly
but requires slightly larger
holes. Experiment to find the
correct drill bit.

**Suggested
Cutters**

Any motif suitable for
Christmas ornaments;
large Easter Eggs or
bunnies; any oversized
cookie.

hese shortcookies taste like sugar cookies but have the texture of dense shortbread. I use this recipe whenever I want a white dough for ornaments. They look great on the tree and will also survive the perils of shipping. Although I've never tried it, I know a woman who used this dough to build a white cookie house instead of the traditional gingerbread one.

Store these cookies in containers that breathe a little (a tin or a box that can be taped closed), since they will lose some of their sturdiness if placed in tightly sealed plastic or glass containers. Kept in a cool, dry place they will last for at least 2 months, so you can bake them well ahead for the holidays.

---

1 cup (2 sticks) salted butter, room temperature	3/4 teaspoon salt
1/2 cup shortening, room temperature	2 1/2 cups all-purpose flour
1 1/4 cups granulated sugar	1 1/2 cups bread flour
1 large egg	1/2 cup brown-rice flour
1 1/2 teaspoons vanilla extract	2—4 tablespoons water, if needed

---

1. With a mixer, cream the butter, shortening, and sugar until fluffy. Add the egg and vanilla extract and beat well.

2. In a mixing bowl, combine the salt, all-purpose flour, bread flour, and brown-rice flour. Stir to blend. Add to the butter mixture and mix on low speed until thoroughly combined. The mixture should come together to form a dough; if it does not, add 2 tablespoons of water and continue mixing until the dough is formed. Pinch a piece of the dough: it should feel soft and pliable. If it cracks and feels dry, add up to an additional 2 tablespoons of water; mix thoroughly. The dough will mass around the beaters and will feel slightly grainy (from the rice flour), but should not be sticky.

3. Turn the dough onto a large piece of plastic wrap or place it in a reclosable plastic bag. Chill in the refrigerator for 15 minutes.

4. Preheat the oven to 375° F. Flour the work surface and rolling pin and remove half the dough from the plastic; rewrap and refrigerate the other half. Roll the dough to a thickness of 5/16 inch and cut into shapes. With a spatula, transfer cookie cutouts to an ungreased baking sheet, keeping them at least 1 inch apart. Form scraps into a ball and chill. Roll and cut remaining dough and scraps.

5. Bake 10–12 minutes, or until the edges just start to brown. Let cool on the baking sheet for 5 minutes and then transfer with a spatula to racks to finish cooling.

 Makes approximately 5 dozen 3-inch cookies or 16 oversized ornaments. This recipe can easily be doubled.

Cookie Bouquets

ou can buy cookie bouquets—fanciful arrangements of cookies-on-a-stick—in cookie shops, but you can make better ones at home.

Containers and Skewers

Choose any container that can be ballasted: a basket, can, or flower pot. Or pick something less obvious—a baseball cap, top hat, or watering can—that will find a second use once the cookies are gone.

Fill the bottom third of the container with beans or glass marbles. Fill the upper two-thirds with styrofoam sheets or a piece of floral oasis (available in craft and flower shops) cut to fit into the container and stacked, if necessary, to hold the cookie flowers firmly. Make sure that the styrofoam or floral oasis fits snugly into the container.

I prefer to use the skewers sold in gourmet shops for barbecuing small items.

Making, Baking, and Arranging the Cookies

Select a dough suitable for ornaments (see pages 126–127, 133–135, and 136–137). Choose large cutters appropriate to the theme of the bouquet, perhaps a baby bottle, rattle, and teddy bear for a newborn. Most bouquets contain between 5 and 7 cookies.

Roll the cookie dough to a thickness of at least

3/8 inch and cut the cookies. Lay the cutouts along one long edge of the baking sheet. Gently insert a thin, sharply pointed wooden skewer into the bottom of each cookie, twisting as you push the skewer up through the dough to the middle of the cookie. To support very large cookies you may need 2 skewers, about 2 inches apart. Using your fingers or a 4-inch lightly floured spatula with a metal blade, gently tamp the front of the cookie where the skewer is inserted, until the dough is smooth.

Bake according to the directions and cool completely on the baking sheets, so that the soft interior of the cookie will harden around the skewer.

After they have cooled completely, decorate the cookies. When the decoration has dried completely, turn the cookie over and coat the back with a single color of royal icing to give a nice finish to the cookie back and help anchor the skewer in place. If a skewer breaks loose, gently reinsert it and repair any damage with a dab of icing. Let the icing dry completely.

Insert the cookies into the weighted container, filling the spaces with colored tissue paper, curly ribbon, artificial Easter grasses, or small candies.

If the bouquet is large, you can create a background with balloons. Blow up 3 balloons, attach them to sticks and balloon cups (available in craft stores) and insert them in the styrofoam.

Making Your Own Cookie Cutters

Although hundreds, maybe thousands, of cookie-cutter shapes are available commercially, you may still yearn for a cutter shaped like your own house, your baby's footprint, or that remarkable dinosaur drawn by your talented 6-year-old. Or you may discover that just when you want to bake pilgrim hats or autumn leaves, every store in town is completely sold out. Making your own metal cookie cutters takes a little skill, but with the right tools and a little patience, you can turn out cutters that are both imaginative and personal.

Although you can make your cutters with or without backs, I prefer the backless ones, because they allow me to see exactly where I am cutting and, in commercial baking, it's important to utilize every last scrap of dough. On the other hand, backs help prevent the cutters from warping and do make an attractive craft project.

Planning Your Design

When planning your design, keep shapes simple and remain open-minded, modifying your plans while your project is still in the design stages: You don't want to make a cutter and then find out that it's difficult to use. You might start by looking at the actual object or a photograph of it.

It's easier to work with a compact shape like an owl than an elongated one like a stork or a giraffe. Avoid tight curves and sharp angles, because the dough will stick in them and tear away from the cookie. A rounded leaf shape is more forgiving than a jagged, pointy one.

In general, keep your cutters fairly small, somewhere between 4 and 6 inches. Larger cutters don't hold their shape as well, and large unbaked cookies can be difficult to handle.

Once you have refined your design, draw it on paper in the size of the finished cutter.

Tools and Supplies

Except for the sheet metal, you should be able to find all these items at your local hardware store.

For backless cutters you will need:

HEAVY-DUTY WORK GLOVES: Preferably of thick, flexible canvas, to protect your hands against cuts and burns.

SHEET METAL: Tin-plated steel is best, but sometimes hard to find. Check the Yellow Pages under "Sheet Metal," or "Metal Fabricators." Galvanized steel is an acceptable substitute, available from some hardware stores, metal fabricators, or heating contractors, who use it for ducts. Some firms that sell hundreds of square yards of metal may balk at selling a few square feet. Whatever metal you choose, ask for 26-, 28-, or 30-gauge metal, firm enough to hold its shape when bent, but easy to cut.

STRAIGHT-BLADED TIN SNIPS: Specialized "scissors" to cut the metal strips.

PLIERS: Needle-nosed pliers and square- or flat-jawed pliers are useful for bending the metal strips into corners and sharp angles. If your design has tight curves, you will need round-jawed pliers as well.

PROPANE TORCH: A small hand-held propane torch for finishing the seam of the cutter. Alternatively, you can finish the seam with a rivet gun.

SOLDER AND FLUX: Use lead-free wire solder. Flux primes the metal surface to receive the solder by preventing the metal from oxidizing when being heated, and allowing the solder to flow freely, thus forming a better bond. Clean the metal with sandpaper before applying flux. Both solder and flux are available at hardware stores.

HAMMER: For pounding the edges of the strips.

SMALL FILE AND FINE SANDPAPER: For smoothing down sharp or rough edges.

Safety Tips

To avoid cutting your fingers, wear work gloves while you prepare the tin strips. Since you will be pressing the cutters into dough with your bare hands, you will have to make a blunt edge, like a hem, on each tin strip by gently folding down a 1/4-inch margin on one long side of the strip. With a hammer, pound the turned-down edge flat against the strip. Alternatively, you may file one edge of the strip until it is no longer sharp. When you solder, be sure to work in a well-ventilated area.

Cutting the Metal

If you cannot get your metal supplier to cut the sheet metal into strips for you, you will have to do it yourself, using straight-bladed tin snips. For 3- to 4-inch cutters, the strips should be about 24 inches long and 3/4 inch wide.

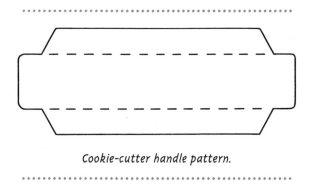

Cookie-cutter handle pattern.

If you plan to make cutters with backs, use your paper pattern and cut the tin back slightly larger than the finished cookie. After you solder the back to the edges, you will trim it down to size. Cutters with backs require handles, so cut out the han-

dles according to the following pattern, adjusting handle length to the size of your design.

Venting the Back

Cutters with backs need air vents, which should be centered on the design if you plan to hang them by the holes. If your pattern is symmetrical, you can determine the center geometrically. If the design is asymmetrical, balance the paper pattern on your fingertips. Mark the location on the pattern and transfer it to the tin. To steady the back, clamp it to a scrap of wood and drill the vent with an electric drill. Smooth the edges of the hole with a round file.

Bending the Tin Edges

You are now ready to form the cutter edges. The bending technique you choose depends on the ins and outs of the design. Begin at one end of the tin strip.

FOR GENTLE CURVES: Shape the tin strip with your fingers.

FOR TIGHTER CURVES: Place the strip between the jaws of your round-jawed pliers. Close the pliers tightly and twist the strip into the desired curve. If you don't have round pliers, bend the tin around a pen, pencil, or other cylindrical object.

FOR CORNERS (RIGHT ANGLES) OR OTHER ABRUPT TURNS: Use square-jawed pliers. Close the pliers tightly, bending the metal into an angle with your free hand.

FOR ACUTE ANGLES: Decide exactly where you want the point of the angle. Squeeze the strip completely closed at this point, using flat-jawed pliers. Then bend it open again to the desired angle.

Continue working around the entire cutter, stopping frequently to check the strip against the paper pattern. When you have completed your design, allow about 1/8 inch of overlap if you plan to solder the seam or 1/4 inch if you plan to use rivets. Cut off the extra tin.

Finishing the Edge Seam

Set the paper pattern on a flat surface and place the cutter on top of it. The cutter edges should touch the surface of the pattern all around the perimeter. If they do not, file or sand down the high spots on the cutter until it rests flat on the pattern.

To finish the seam with rivets. Hold the 2 ends of the cutter firmly together and close the seam with

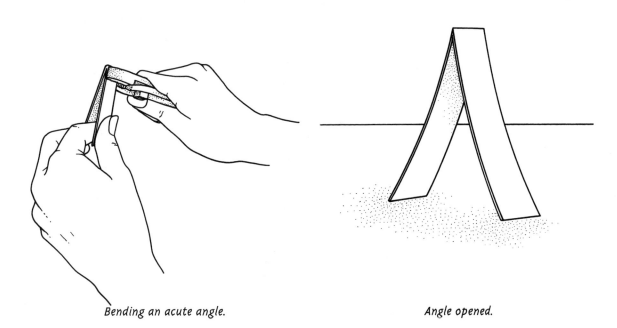

Bending an acute angle.

Angle opened.

2 or 3 small rivets. Be sure to place the rivets close to the edge of the seam so that it will close tightly, without an extra flap of tin sticking up.

To finish by soldering. Set the propane torch carefully on a level surface or secure it in a vice to prevent it from tipping over. Turn it on to a low setting. Wearing protective gloves, close the seam with one hand and unwind about an inch of solder from the roll. This job is a lot easier with two people, one to hold the seam, the other to manipulate the solder.

Sandpaper the seam edge you plan to solder and brush flux on the sandpapered area. Heat the edges of the seam 5 to 10 seconds. Touch the solder

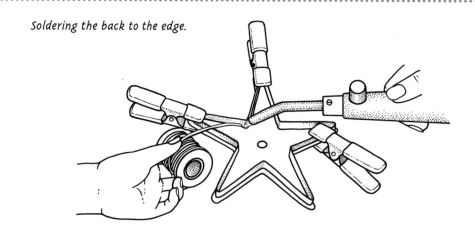

Soldering the back to the edge.

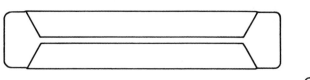

Handle with sides bent inwards.

Handle curved.

to the seam and continue heating until the solder melts and flows. The unrolled solder should melt off the spool. If necessary, turn and tilt the cutter so that the liquid solder flows to close the seam completely.

After the solder has cooled, file the seam smooth with a small file. Wash and scrub the cutter with dish soap.

Set the finished cookie cutter on a flat, level surface to make sure that all the edges touch the surface. If the cutter has warped, put a medium-weight book on top. Leave the book in place for 24 hours to season the cutter and return it to its original, unwarped shape. If you are making a cutter with a back, you will now attach the back and handle.

Soldering the Back to the Edge

This job takes more skill than just closing the edge seam, but with practice you will be able to attach the back without gaps or irregular blobs of solder. Before you begin, make sure the back and the edge piece are both as flat as possible. Clamp the back to the edge, using spring clamps.

Set the propane torch on low. Brush flux on the joint, working around the perimeter in 3- or 4-inch segments. Unroll solder from the spool. With the torch set on low, heat the joint until the flux is hot and touch the unrolled solder to the heated seam.

If the metal is the correct temperature, the solder will melt immediately. If the metal is too cool, the solder won't flow. If it is too hot, it will turn red or burn the flux. Should that happen, cool the metal, wash it, and try again. As your soldering skills improve, you should be able to direct the torch along the seam ahead of the wire solder, heating the next segment so that the melted solder flows into it. When you have finished the seam, wash the cutter.

Making the Handle

Bend back the edges of the handle along the dotted lines. You can put the handle in a vise and use the edges of the jaws as a guide. Gently hammer down the edges so that they touch at the center.

Using pliers, shape the handle into an arch. Bend back the end tabs so that they will rest evenly on a flat surface. Clamp the handle to the back and solder in place.

Finishing the Cutter

Using tin snips, trim off the overhang so that the back fits the cutter edge. If some angles are too sharp to cut precisely (the "V" between a gingerbread boy's legs), cut straight across the angle. Smooth down any sharp edges with a file.

Mail Order Sources for Equipment and Ingredients

Bates Nut Farm
  15954 Woods Valley Road
  Valley Center, California 92082
  (619) 749-3333; outside California:
  (800) 642-0348

Shelled nuts, including black walnuts, dried fruits.
  Catalogue available.

Bridge Kitchenware
  214 East 52nd Street
  New York, New York 10022
  (212) 688-4220

Baking sheets, decorating bags, icing tips.
  More than 600 different cutters including
  sets (round, fluted), novelty items (fire
hydrants, 5 different Christmas trees). Call for
catalogue.

Country Kitchen Products
  3225 Wells Street
  Fort Wayne, Indiana 46808
  (219) 482-4835

In business for more than 20 years. Food colorings,
  especially Luster Dust, a dry coloring which
  imparts a metallic sheen, available in edible
  and nonedible forms. Also Wilton products,
  cutters, and miscellaneous baking and
  decorating supplies.

Dean & DeLuca

560 Broadway

New York, New York 10012

(212) 431-1691

Baking pans, utensils, and other elegant cookware. The store, in SoHo, has a dazzling display of first-class foods.

Hammer Song

221 South Potomac Street

Boonsboro, Maryland 21713

(301) 432-4320

Cookie cutters; catalogue available.

Harry and David

P.O. Box 712

Medford, Oregon 97051-0719

Customer Service: (800) 345-5655

Known for their fruit baskets and cheese cakes, which can be ordered by mail, Harry and David has outlets that sell shelled nuts and other items not listed in the catalogues. Call customer service for location of outlets.

Little Fox Factory

931 Marion Road

Bucyrus, Ohio 44820

(419) 562-5420

Cookie cutters and information about the Cookie Cutter Collectors club. More than 15 varieties of dog-shaped cutters.

Munnell & Sherrill Industrial Supply

1163 N.E. 63rd Street

P.O. Box 13249

Portland, Oregon 97213

(503) 281-0021

Sanalite plastic sheets, custom fitted to your needs.

New York Cake & Baking Center

56 West 22nd Street

New York, New York 10010

(212) 675-2253 or (800) 94-CAKE-9

Cookie cutters, dragées, paste dyes, ingredients, and baking sheets. Catalogue available.

Parrish Decorating Supplies, Inc.

314 West 58th Street

Los Angeles, California 90037

(213) 750-7650;

outside California (800) 736-8443

Cookie cutters, paste dyes, and heavy aluminum, dull-finished baking sheets.

Purple Puma Cookie Company

R.R. #1, Box 1420

Gilmanton Iron Works

New Hampshire 03837

(603) 267-6036

Part of Bark and Bradley, a company that designs and manufactures cookie cutters and markets herbal seasoning packets. Wholesale only. For retail, see Zeb's General Store.

Santa Papers by Hunter, Inc.

P.O. Box 26016

Fairview Park, Ohio 44126

(216) 331-0327

Owners Karen Riddlebaugh Hunter and Mary Jane Riddlebaugh sell cookie cutters, as well as decorative papers that adhere to baked, cooled cookies with a little jelly. These papers are printed with soybean-based ink, approved by the FDA.

Sur la Table

84 Pike Street

Pike Place Farmers' Market

Seattle, Washington 98101

(800) 243-0852

Has a specialized baking catalogue. Cutters, stamps, molds, pans, instant-read

thermometers, decorating tips and bags, paste dyes, rolling pin rings, marble rolling pins.

Sweet Celebrations

7009 Washington Avenue South

Edina, Minnesota 55439

(800) 328-6722

Colored sugars, sprinkles, edible glitter, icing flowers, sugar flowers, wide variety of cookie cutters. In 1994 this company bought the assets of Maid of Scandinavia and now markets their bakers' and confectioners' supplies and equipment.

White Lily Foods Company

P.O. Box 871

Knoxville, Tennessee 37901

(423) 546-5511

Flours, including my favorite unbleached all-purpose flour, and soft wheat flour.

Williams-Sonoma

Mail Order Department

P. O. Box 7456

San Francisco, California 94120-7456

(800) 541-2233

Catalogue changes monthly, features seasonally appropriate cookie cutters, stamps, molds.

Ingredients also change seasonally and include flours, oils, and chocolate.

Wilton Enterprises

22440 West 75th Street
Woodridge, Illinois 60517
(630) 963-7100 or (800) 794-5866

An important resource for beginning and advanced cookie decorators. Baking pans, cutters, icing tips, and bags. Instructional books and kits. Ingredients including glitter, sprinkles, other icing decorations. Catalogue available.

Yvonne's Kitchen Shoppe

1085 Rogue Valley Mall
1600 North Riverside
Medford, Oregon 97504
(541) 776-9845

Cookie cutters, stamps, molds, rolling pin guides, and ingredients including Guittard's Dutch-process cocoa in bulk.

Zeb's General Store

P.O. Box 1915
North Conway, New Hampshire 03860
(800) 676-9294, or (603) 356-9294

Offers New England products, including maple sugars and gift baskets. Is the retail mail order source for Bark and Bradley products, including individual cutters in many designs and miniature cutter collections (endangered species, great American desert, Noah's ark, a Nutcracker Christmas, and an Advent cookie calendar) and art dough collections for making cookie ornaments. Call for brochure, which includes Bark and Bradley catalogue.

Mail Order Sources for Decorated Cookies

Aunt Gussie's Cookies

38 Irving Place
Garfield, New Jersey 07026
(800) 4A- COOKI

Owners Marilyn and David Caine offer large sugar cookies, rugelah, cracker flat breads, and biscotti. Wholesale and retail. Brochure and price list.

Baked Ideas

450 Broadway
New York, New York 10013
(212) 925-9097

Owned by Patty Paige, this firm sells hand-decorated gingerbread cookies in many different designs. Wholesale and retail. Brochure and price list.

Goose Hill Farm

9452-A Deschutes Road
Palo Cedro, CA 96073
(888) 547-3647

Debbie Greenfield, owner, offers gift-boxed stamped Scandinavian shortbreads; the raised designs are hand-painted with edible dyes and dusted with FDA-approved Luster Dust. Designs for all seasons. Brochure and price list.

"O My Goodness!"

910 Sherwood Drive
Suite #23
Lake Bluff, Illinois 60044
(847) 735-9890

Hand-decorated butter cookies, sold in cellophane bags and tied off with tulle. Personalized cookies. Minimum order.

Sarah Lingwood's Kitchens

1116 34th Street
Anacortes, Washington 98221
(541) 846-6890

Gingerbread cookies. Wholesale orders only.

Sugarbakers' Cookies

P.O. Box 325
Williams, Oregon 97544
Orders: (541) 846-6890
Special sales and design work: (541) 779-7967

Part of The Joy of Cookies. Hand-decorated gingerbread and shortbread cookies for wholesale, retail, and gift basket market. Cookies individually shrink-wrapped. Also cookie ornaments, personalized orders. Color brochures available. Minimum order.

Index

154

158